A Port in Global Capitalism

Through a study of the port district of Rio de Janeiro and its history, from its emergence as a major slave market to its modern-day incarnation as a hub of tourism, real estate and financial speculation, this book examines the different dimensions of the manner in which capitalism expands its global process of accumulation to incorporate spaces not yet integrated into chains of value production. As such, it sheds new light on the use of explicit non-economic violence on the part of capitalist expansion, in the form of colonial or imperial policies, plundering or legal forms of expropriation. As such, it will appeal to sociologists, historians, economists, legal scholars and political theorists with interests in capitalism and inequalities.

Sérgio Costa is Professor of Sociology at Freie Universität Berlin, Germany. Trained in Economics and Sociology in Brazil and Germany, his main research fields are social inequality, conviviality and difference and postcolonial theories.

Guilherme Leite Gonçalves is Professor of Sociology of Law at the Rio de Janeiro State University, Brazil. He is interested in social theory, particularly in issues of law, social control and inequalities.

Entangled Inequalities: Exploring Global Asymmetries
Series Editor: Sérgio Costa
Freie Universität Berlin, Germany

https://www.routledge.com/Entangled-Inequalities-Exploring-Global-Asym
metries/book-series/ASHSER1413

Departing from classical approaches to the study of social inequalities between individuals and social classes within particular national settings, this series emphasises the production and reproduction of inequalities across borders as well as the multiplicity of categories – whether 'race', 'sex' or 'nationality' amongst others – according to which contemporary inequalities are shaped.

Entangled Inequalities constitutes a forum and a catalyst for discussing recent advancements in inequality research from a transnational, global and intersectional perspective, highlighting the fact that social inequalities are always the product of both global interpenetrations and of complex intersections between different social categorisations. The series therefore welcomes monographs and edited volumes across the social sciences that deal with inequalities from an 'entangled' perspective – with an intersectional or a transnational focus, or both.

Titles in this series

A Moment of Equality for Latin America?
Barbara Fritz and Lena Lavinas

Social Mobilization, Global Capitalism and Struggles over Food
Renata Motta

Reducing Inequality in Latin America
María Fernanda Valdés Valencia

Global Entangled Inequalities
Elizabeth Jelin, Renata C. Motta, Sérgio Costa

A Port in Global Capitalism
Sérgio Costa and Guilherme Leite Gonçalves

A Port in Global Capitalism
Unveiling Entangled Accumulation in
Rio de Janeiro

**Sérgio Costa and
Guilherme Leite Gonçalves**

LONDON AND NEW YORK

First published 2020
by Routledge
2 Park Square, Milton Park, Abingdon, Oxon OX14 4RN

and by Routledge
52 Vanderbilt Avenue, New York, NY 10017

Routledge is an imprint of the Taylor & Francis Group, an informa business

© 2020 Sérgio Costa & Guilherme Leite Gonçalves

The right of Sérgio Costa & Guilherme Leite Gonçalves to be identified as authors of this work has been asserted by them in accordance with sections 77 and 78 of the Copyright, Designs and Patents Act 1988.

All rights reserved. No part of this book may be reprinted or reproduced or utilised in any form or by any electronic, mechanical, or other means, now known or hereafter invented, including photocopying and recording, or in any information storage or retrieval system, without permission in writing from the publishers.

Trademark notice: Product or corporate names may be trademarks or registered trademarks, and are used only for identification and explanation without intent to infringe.

British Library Cataloguing-in-Publication Data
A catalog record for this book is available from the British Library

Library of Congress Cataloging-in-Publication Data
Names: Costa, Sérgio, 1962- author. | Gonçalves, Guilherme Leite, author.
Title: A port in global capitalism: unveiling entangled accumulation in
Rio de Janeiro/Sérgio Costa, Guilherme Leite Gonçalves.
Description: Milton Park, Abingdon, Oxon; New York, NY: Routledge,
2019. | Series: Entangled inequalities: exploring global asymmetries |
Includes bibliographical references and index. |
Identifiers: LCCN 2019027775 | ISBN 9780367340964 (hardback) |
ISBN 9780429323898 (ebook)
Subjects: LCSH: Rio de Janeiro (Brazil)–Economic conditions. |
Harbors–Brazil–Rio de Janeiro. | Capitalism–Brazil–Rio de Janeiro.
Classification: LCC HC189.R4 C68 2019 | DDC 330.981/53–dc23
LC record available at https://lccn.loc.gov/2019027775

ISBN: 978-0-367-34096-4 (hbk)
ISBN: 978-0-429-32389-8 (ebk)

Typeset in Times
by Deanta Global Publishing Services, Chennai, India

Contents

	Introduction	1
1	From primitive accumulation to entangled accumulation: developments in the Marxist theory of capitalist expansion	6
2	Port, capital and the capital city	25
3	Capitalism and slavery in the port of Rio de Janeiro	34
4	From the first attempts at industrialisation to financialisation: 'Little Africa' vs Porto Maravilha	57
5	Crisis anchored at the port	75
	Conclusions	96
	Bibliography	101
	Index	113

Introduction

The port district was one of the areas most affected by the urban interventions demanded for the reception of the Olympics, which took place in August 2016 in Rio de Janeiro. Until the 1990s, the area was generally viewed by business groups, politicians, investors and the mainstream media as a devalued and degraded space, one which was isolated from the rest of the city. In fact, the entire area had low market value and was of little interest for real estate investments, commercial transactions and services. Even the port itself was of little significance when compared to other Brazilian ports. For all intents and purposes, the region was located 'outside' the process of capitalist accumulation.

This situation changed dramatically in November 2009, about a month after Rio de Janeiro was chosen to host the Olympics, ahead of the finalists Tokyo, Madrid and Chicago. At the time, the choice of Rio de Janeiro as the first South American host of the Olympics in history raised the suspicion of specialists and competitors regarding the honesty of the process. More than a year after the Olympic Games took place, it became evident that these suspicions were not unfounded. In 2017, after a wide investigation known as 'Operation Unfair Play', the Brazilian police arrested the president of the Brazilian Olympic Committee, Carlos Nuzman, a lawyer and relatively successful former volleyball player. He was accused of illicit enrichment as well as coordinating the transfer of funds to purchase the votes of members of the International Olympic Committee (IOC) in favour of Rio de Janeiro in the weeks preceding the 2009 decision (Watts, 2017).

About a month after Rio de Janeiro was chosen to host the Olympics, the Porto Maravilha (Marvellous Port) project was made public. This project catalysed promotional campaigns and economic, political and cultural expectations, restructuring the entire port district for value creation. The former mayor of Rio de Janeiro, Eduardo Paes, triumphantly announced in the 18th edition of the Porto Maravilha magazine that advances had been made in the 'revitalisation' and 'regeneration' of the nearly 5 million square metres in the port district of the city. The mayor echoed the general tone adopted in the dissemination of the broad plan of urban intervention unleashed in 2009. To him, the project would 'regain' for public use 'a central area of the city with immense historical importance', which had become 'a demographic vacuum' after 'decades of degradation' (Paes, 2015: 2).

2 Introduction

Inhabitants of the port district, representatives of social movements and various experts – even those that support the project – are unanimous in rejecting the idea that the area in question was a vacuum of vitality and sociability. They highlight the presence of residents as well as the existence of diverse cultural activities, which are quite developed in the region. On top of all of this, it was obvious that the space being 'revalued' was charged with history and ancestral references.

In 2011, when the subsoil was perforated for the infrastructure projects linked to the urban reforms of the port district, a true archaeological treasure was discovered. At first casually, later professionally by a team of archaeologists and Afro-Brazilian preachers, the vestiges of the old port from different periods were unearthed. The findings joined others that had been recovered in past years in the port district. Not only were mortal remains discovered, but also a vast heritage of material culture linked to persons wrenched from Africa and brought to be sold as slaves in Rio de Janeiro. In this area, a variety of activities and functions had been in place at the turn of the 19th century for the purpose of selling human beings: the 'meat market', as the spot dedicated to the sale of enslaved persons was known, a lazarette, the landing dock, and Cemetery of Pretos Novos (in English 'New Blacks' – meaning the newly arrived enslaved Africans), where Africans who had perished during the passage of the Atlantic or at the market itself were buried (Lima et al., 2016). The cultural value of the archaeological collection found in the area known as *Cais do Valongo* led UNESCO to name it a World Heritage Site in July 2017 (Londoño, 2017).

In the full context of neo-developmentalist euphoria that took hold of Brazil at the beginning of the 2010s, the material and discursive construction of the port surroundings as an economic and social vacuum that was (expected) to be occupied and civilised seemed an unprecedented phenomenon. In fact, it was not. It was simply a new backdrop for a story that has continued to *repeat itself* for centuries. In its various phases, the port of Rio de Janeiro has been traversed by the different watersheds of the capitalist dynamic which, according to the necessities of accumulation, sometimes repel, sometimes attract and integrate spaces, processes and relations to the market. This is thus a story marked by actors, forces and social pressures that alternate in a continuous movement of commodification, decommodification and recommodification of the space contiguous to the port, including, along with the space itself, the bodies, goods, products and activities that inhabit it.

In line with the recent literature that recovers and broadens the discussion about primitive accumulation and capitalist expropriation initially developed by Karl Marx (1906 [1867]), the present book argues that the rhetorical establishment of a demographic vacuum in the centre of Rio de Janeiro is part of the process that connects commodified and non-commodified territories, a condition for the creation of capitalist value. However, the goal of this book goes a step further. It seeks to illustrate that the processes of incorporation, decoupling and reincorporation of the port district into the dynamic of accumulation have systematically accompanied the history of the area from the creation of the port at the end of the 16th century.

Introduction 3

Since Rosa Luxemburg (2003 [1913]), Marxist political economists have been aware of the fact that the accumulation of capital is not limited to a purely economic process between the owners of the means of production and workers in spaces where surplus value is produced. On the contrary, as just one part of surplus value can be appropriated in this internal circuit, the system must resort to a 'non-capitalist exterior' to completely appropriate it. For this purpose, capitalism makes use of open, explicit and non-economic violence, such as colonial or imperial expansion, plundering, bloody legislation, etc. In other words, the same logic of primitive accumulation, as described by Marx, has been repeating itself throughout the course of capitalist history. This recurrence is in fact required by capitalist expansion itself, which must commodify not yet commodified spaces.

The port district of Rio de Janeiro represents a sort of metonymy of global capitalism inasmuch as the various historical phases of capitalist development can be reconstructed along the alternating cycles through which the port region has been integrated into and uncoupled from the processes that transform socially constructed spaces into commodities. It is thus a miniature of the metamorphoses of capitalist expansion itself. Given its privileged location as a point of entry for commodities and a space dedicated to the provision of diverse services, the port is a key setting for the reproduction of Brazil's processes of integration into global capitalism in its various stages.

In the first chapter of the book, we briefly reconstruct the most recent developments in Marxist theory on capitalist expansion, in particular, those that indicate that mechanisms like the ones Marx described as primitive or original accumulation continue to be central for the reproduction of capitalism. Using the concept of entangled accumulation, we seek to articulate and expand on these theoretical developments. The second chapter explores the relations between the port and the city in order to reveal the different processes and mechanisms that associate port and city to capitalist accumulation. Chapters 3 and 4 reconstruct different phases in the history of the port area of Rio de Janeiro to illustrate the most important movements in the pattern of accumulation observed there, taking into consideration different phases in the life of the port and the city: mercantilist accumulation, the nascent process of industrialisation and finally the recent attempts to financialise the district. To delimit the vast pertinent material for the analysis developed here, relevant legal changes are used as orientation for the variations in the pattern of accumulation verified in each period.

The economic and political crisis, in which Brazil has been immersed since 2014, has generated devastating effects for the Porto Maravilha project. Planed in a period of economic euphoria, the project depends on the increasing interest of investors in paying for the right to construct in the port area. However, the crisis has led to shrinking expectations of profit and to the suspension of investments in the port area. It is only possible to make profits through new expropriations (of state resources, workers' funds, etc.), which represent again a commodification of fields not yet completed integrated into the circuits of capital accumulation. The current moment of crisis and reinvention of finance accumulation is discussed in the Chapter 5. Lastly, the conclusion synthesises links between the theoretical

4   *Introduction*

developments and the case studied and discusses the issues that remain open as a possible agenda for future research.

This book was born as an attempt to use the Porto Maravilha project to elaborate on a paper on the ongoing process of primitive accumulation, presented at the Congress of the Latin American Studies Association in San Juan, Puerto Rico, in May 2015. Since then, the original essay has continued to grow, somewhat of its own accord, into an academic article and a number of contributions for the critical press. Even if the central argument developed in this book is rather ambitious, the current study maintains, both in its form and in the scope of the covered literature, the modesty of the first draft. If the book has any merit, it is certainly not that it makes an unprecedented and original contribution to the contemporary debate, which is already very dense and diverse on the thesis of ongoing primitive accumulation and the notion of capitalist expropriation. The purpose of the book is not historiographic either. The literature on the history of the port and the city of Rio de Janeiro, as voluminous as it is sophisticated, is used in a specific and selective manner to highlight just some of the aspects and debates that enable us to elucidate the argument developed here.

Instead, this book attempts to make a contribution of another nature. It rejects the current orientalisms and occidentalisms even among critical authors, who reclaim the concept of primitive accumulation to study the ills of neoliberal capitalism. By not reflecting upon these Eurocentric presuppositions, these authors make the mistake of believing in the existence of a European predecessor and a peripheral successor in the history of capitalism. The links between Rio de Janeiro and its port and the European metropolis show with disconcerting clarity that, from January 1502, when the Portuguese navigator Gaspar de Lemos first sighted the Bay of Guanabara believing to have arrived at the mouth of a large river, this piece of the earth was irreversibly integrated into the (pre)history of modernity and capitalism. In effect, from the 16th century on, the port and the city became one of the knots in a web of relations and flows of commodities and persons that, for the fortune of a select few and the misfortune of countless others, irrevocably entangled and brought Europe, the Americas, Africa and, as will be shown, even Asia closer. This is the main message this book wants to convey.

As with any academic research, the present book, though written by two authors, is the product of dialogue with many others. Firstly, we thank those present at the meeting in San Juan, in particular Lena Lavinas, who discussed the paper with her unique generosity and brilliance, providing us with invaluable comments for developing our reflection. The same gratitude is extended to our colleagues who participated in the Colloquium 'Marxistische Theorie und kritische Soziologie' at Friedrich-Schiller-Universität Jena in January 2017, when we received valuable critiques and comments, in particular from Klaus Dörre, whose contribution and work were fundamental for the construction of our argument. The same is also valid for the participants of the Conference 'Marx and the Global South', which took place in Bremen in May 2018. We would also like to express our gratitude to Virginia Fontes for reading and pointing out her

Introduction 5

observations to one of our versions to the critical press; her theory of expropriation constitutes another cornerstone of our formulation.

We also thank Rafael Cardoso, whose competent criticism and thorough references allowed us to correct inaccuracies in the first version of our book; Krista Lillemets, for her, as always, pertinent and useful comments; and Paulo Fontes, who was a safe haven of indications for navigating the research and historiographic literature. This book has been simultaneously written in both languages, Portuguese and English. Iasmin Goes and Clay Johnson translated most chapters; also Diego Rivas and Rositsa Mahdi supported us on this.

The selfless assistance we received from our colleagues does not of course make them in any way responsible for possible errors in this book. These lie exclusively in our own hands. Finally, we would like to highlight that our present research was, in its different phases, financed by the network *desiguALdades. net* based at the Freie Universität Berlin, the Maria Sibylla Merian International Centre Conviviality-Inequality (Mecila), the Alexander von Humboldt Foundation, the Faculty of Social Sciences at the University Kassel and the Centre *Postwachstumsgesellschaften* of the Friedrich Schiller University Jena.

We wish you a stimulating read, and we hope to receive many critiques and comments that will allow us to continue reconstructing and retelling, in a more accurate way, the stories of entangled accumulation that perpetually repeat themselves and that capitalism and nationalism insist on concealing.

1 From primitive accumulation to entangled accumulation

Developments in the Marxist theory of capitalist expansion[1]

Various critical studies on capitalism, including the theory of regulation (Boyer and Saillard, 2005) and of crisis (Harvey, 2005), all have a common thread: they recognise a continuous driving process behind capitalist accumulation. During a given period, capitalism produces the material conditions that guarantee its expansion and, consequently, ensure its preservation as a mode of production in the subsequent phase of expansion. That is, capitalism is a dynamic formation which depends on constant pressure for growth and thus must perpetually overcome its self-imposed limitations generated during the reproduction of capital. In a nutshell, capitalism is a machinery that is highly sensitive to any limits to expansion – limits which, when reached, activate processes that change its skin in order to generate a new cycle of dynamic stability, expansion and growth (Dörre, Lessenich and Rosa, 2015: 28).

This process of continual expansion, although empirically evident, is not trivial from the analytical point of view. Understanding its entire breadth and complexity demands reconstructing some of the basic concepts of Marxist political economy. This is precisely the aim of the present chapter. Initially, we recover variations and reformulations which the concept of primitive accumulation has passed through since Marx reflected upon it. Then we discuss a less explored aspect of the Marxist political economy, namely, the role played by regulatory instruments in constructing the necessary conditions of capitalist accumulation. At the close of the chapter, the different arguments developed here are crystallised around the concept of entangled accumulation.

Conceptual precursor of the notion of primitive accumulation

In Marx (1906 [1867]: 786), primitive accumulation is treated as an original act prior to the movement, which is the central trademark of capitalism, namely, the uninterrupted circuit in which money is transformed into capital and by means of which surplus value is created, and vice versa. Thus, according to Marx (1906 [1867]: 507, 786), there exists a previous accumulation that is the point of departure for the capitalist mode of production. As the premise for capitalist production is the transformation of material or immaterial goods into value, which is only possible by means of the 'complete separation of the labourers from all property

From primitive to entangled accumulation   7

in the means by which they can realise their labour', Marx concludes that primitive accumulation is the 'historical process of divorcing the producer from the means of production'.

Primitive accumulation is thus an act of expropriation at two levels: in the spaces in Europe, where industrial capitalism originally emerged, direct producers were stripped of the means of guaranteeing their own physical and social reproduction. The immediate consequence is the creation of a mass of workers who are 'free' to sell their labour. Together with the separation of producers and means of production in Europe, capitalist expansion was fed by colonial expansion and concentration of merchant capital. For Marx (1906 [1867]: 786) both processes are part of a global process of accumulation. It is also not a glorious liberation as it is often described by the classics of political economy, mainly Adam Smith. On the contrary, it involves imperial conquests, enslavement, robbery, murder and regulatory interventions, that is, non-economic violence. As a result, the ownership of the means of production is monopolised by a small group capable of purchasing labour-power that is available on the market on the market and thus able to initiate the process of value creation.

Building on the concept 'previous accumulation' coined by A. Smith, Marx (1906 [1867]: 741) refers to this process as the so-called 'primitive accumulation' to highlight both: the violent character of accumulation and its persistence in the history of capitalism. Throughout the development of capitalism, the exploitation of the worker has become a 'natural law of production', according to which the workers are permanently reproduced as workers, or sellers of their labour-power, while the owners of the means of production are lifted to the condition of appropriators of surplus value.

Although the logic of this economic law requires the simulated violence of the fetishism, Marx (1906 [1867]: 809) argues that, in capitalist normality, '[d]irect force, outside economic conditions, is of course still used, but only exceptionally'. Such 'exceptionality' is qualitative rather than quantitative. When capitalist production is already established, Marx (1906 [1867]: 834) affirms that expropriation does not cease but is reproduced on an ever-increasing scale, according to specific forms of concentration of capital and private property. That is, the logic of the violent, original or primitive accumulation is repeated, now as a continuous expropriation, a condition for the accumulation of capital to concentrate more and more.

Luxemburg, for her part, identifies this phenomenon as a determining factor in the development of capitalism itself. She argues that only a part of the movement of accumulation is realised in a purely economic process between capitalists and workers where surplus value is produced (Luxemburg, 2003 [1913]). In this context, as she states, 'peace, property and equality prevail', that is, 'the right of ownership changes in the course of accumulation into appropriation of other people's property, how commodity exchange turns into exploitation and equality becomes class-rule' (Luxemburg, 2003 [1913]: 432).

However, just a relative and limited part of surplus value can be appropriated in this internal circuit, that is, at the site of its production. For this reason,

8 From primitive to entangled accumulation

Luxemburg (2003 [1913]: 348) contends that the system must always resort to a non-capitalist 'exterior' in order to appropriate the surplus value completely. This other dimension of accumulation operates on the global stage and cannot be scrutinised by means of social forms of dissimulation. On the contrary, in the flow between capital and non-capitalist spaces, the methods employed do not dispense explicit violence in the form of 'colonial policy, an international loan system – a policy of spheres of interest – and war' (Luxemburg, 2003[1913]: 432).

Using Luxemburg's observations as a point of departure, Harvey (2004: 74 ff) develops the argument that accumulation based on violence is not an 'original stage' or a past act, but a process which permanently repeats itself in the course of capitalist development. For this reason, he deemed the phenomenon 'accumulation by dispossession'. Harvey (2004: 64) contends that '[o]veraccumulation within a given territorial system' is the result of the excess of labour, in the form of unemployment, and of capital, too, as materialised in the abundance of goods that cannot be sold without losses as well as the destruction of productive potentiality and the excess of capital lacking any possibilities of becoming profitable. According to Harvey, this surplus can be absorbed either by employing temporal adjustments ('investment in long-term capital projects') or spatial adjustments ('opening up of new markets, new production capacities and new resource, social and labour possibilities') or by combining both (Harvey, 2004: 64). When these temporal–spatial adjustments are not possible by means of 'expanded reproduction on a sustained basis', Harvey (2004: 63–64) claims that accumulation resorts to other means, namely, accumulation by dispossession.

It is thus a 'vulture capitalism' that recovers the predatory practices and political violence of primitive accumulation as described by Marx (Harvey, 2004: 72). Dörre (2015: 30) shows that, implicitly, Harvey does not reduce accumulation by dispossession exclusively to 'cannibalistic', 'fraudulent' or 'predatory' practices as characterised by Marx and Luxemburg. Such practices may or may not manifest themselves in contemporary forms of capitalist expansion. The specific and decisive factor is that the accumulation of capital always occurs via different means of state intervention. This is precisely the point of departure for Dörre's studies on the capitalist expropriation of space (*kapitalistische Landnahme*).[2] His premise is that 'capitalism is a self- negating market economy' (Dörre, 2015: 19). For Dörre (2015: 13), liberal economic thinking, based on the idea of competition and efficiency as the absence of duress and regulation, masks both the capitalist dynamic and the political-state dimension of its very project. It is true that orthodox liberalism questions the view of the state as a forum that determines the rules of the game and an arbiter who ensures the application of such rules. But it is also true that market actors operate according to mechanisms of cooperation (as opposed to competition) and depend on predictability and experience with elementary social stabilities in order to operate.

For this reason, Dörre (2015: 13) argues that the thesis of a pure market economy performs *ideological* functions by veiling the relations of power and politics that permeate the relations of exchange, as well as *strategic* relationships, seeing as in situations of crisis, one can always blame the crisis on the errors of existing

From primitive to entangled accumulation 9

regulation and call for waves of deregulation, movements which necessarily constitute regulation in other terms. In this way, political-regulatory intervention, whether unleashed in the name of regulation or, paradoxically, in the name of deregulation, is a constant in the development of capitalism (Dörre, 2015: 15).

Echoing Harvey, the model of capitalist expropriation developed by Dörre postulates that the accumulation of capital always stumbles upon temporal–spatial barriers, which must be overcome for its continuity. He presents the idea that it is impossible to completely appropriate surplus value in the place of production, that is, there are limits to the capacity to create demand and supply expanding economies if these remain restricted to already commodified spaces. In this way, Dörre demonstrates that the accumulation of capital demands new non-commodified territories for its perpetuation. These territories can then supply new resources, raw materials and labour markets and also create new consumption needs (Dörre et al., 2015: 27). Dörre assumes Harvey's argument that non-commodified spaces are not limited to non-capitalist territories and relations of production. If they were, the process of capital expansion would be an irreversible phenomenon which would tend to exhaust itself. On the contrary, the permanent necessity of overcoming the bounds of accumulation leads capitalism to produce non-commodified spaces which it subsequently expropriates. Hence, in Dörre's words, 'the chain of potential Landnahmen is veritably endless' (Dörre et al., 2015: 28).

The idea that capitalist accumulation is sustained by a continuous and permanent creation and expropriation of non-commodified spaces finds support and empirical inspiration in the move from Fordism to financial capitalism. Its axiom is a positive interpretation of the post-war period spanning until the 1970s – the *Trente Glorieuses* – in Western Europe, Japan and the USA. By investing in infrastructure, qualification of the labour-power, and factories and machines, Fordism created the conditions for economic exploitation in a given space, as Harvey (2005: 147 ss) shows. These investments could only be amortised in the long term, a fact which made the state the key for movements of capital. By absorbing excess through investments in public goods in long cycles, the state created a strategy to disarm the dispositive of overaccumulation (Dörre, 2015: 29).

Dörre (2015: 29) understands state investment in the production of public goods as the formation of an 'exterior' which, despite contributing to the execution of economic activities, is initially 'inaccessible for private accumulation'. This sets the stage for a new capitalist takeover. In other words, as public investments (in roads, airports, the energy supply, telecommunications, health care, etc.) are amortised, they become an obstacle for the valorisation of capital; thus the production of these goods and services gradually passes into the hands of private market actors. When the control of goods and services which were previously produced by the state falls into the hands of private companies, new fields open themselves up to the investment of surplus capital, which can then be converted into a means of surplus production. Yet, this is only possible because the relations of property have changed and, consequently, the past producers of public services (namely, state agencies) have been separated from the means of production which, for their part, have passed into the hands of private companies via privatisation.

10   *From primitive to entangled accumulation*

Along with privatisations, Harvey (2005: 147 ff) considers financialisation to be one of the central mechanisms of contemporary processes of accumulation by dispossession in the context of neoliberal capitalism.[3] Financialisation, understood by Harvey as the exponential increase of financial transactions from the 1980s onwards, has created new instruments of dispossession of families and individuals, promoting a redistribution of wealth from the bottom to the top of the social pyramid. The most evident case of this is the real estate bubbles that occurred at the end of the 2000s in the United States and Spain. These bubbles brought an unprecedented transfer of savings from middle- and low-income families to financial institutions and causing these families' future to surrender their income to pay off the debts they had incurred – debts which would continue existing even after the financial and mortgage-related goods have been handed over to the financial system. Something similar has been occurring with many pension funds which, after successive losses in their financial applications, are no longer capable of guaranteeing the livelihood of pensioners who have contributed to the respective funds their whole lives. In the same way, the recurring manipulation in transactions based on stock values is a mechanism which, in the process of financialisation, has 'brought immense wealth to a few at the expense of the many' (Harvey, 2006: 154).

Dörre (2015: 30 ss) also studies financialisation, treating it as a new capitalist social formation characterised by neoliberal politics of austerity and the precarisation of labour. Dörre's merit consists in conferring macrosociological features to the thesis advanced by Harvey. That is, grounded in the postulate that capitalism involves the permanent expansion of capital accumulation via the expropriation of non-commodified spaces (whether they previously existed or were actively produced), Dörre (2015: 28) deduces that capitalism functions on the basis of an inside–outside dialectic, according to which the limits of its internal capacity of accumulation demand the permanent expropriation of a non-commodified 'exterior' (i.e. territorial and social spaces or spheres which do not yet produce primarily value).

The main problem of Harvey's and Dörre's models is the risk of presenting expropriation or dispossession as a process operating outside of capitalism (Callinicus, 2009). As already seen in Marx's work, the concentration and centralisation of capital itself demands permanent violence against living labour. In this sense, expropriation cannot be seen as a distinct dynamic, but as an integral part of capital accumulation itself. Pradella (2014) shows that this incorporation of primitive accumulation into the development of capitalism is related to the concentration of money worldwide. At the same time as this process contributes to the constitution of British industry, it transforms global production relations. If from a theoretical point of view this means that Marx had already included primitive accumulation into his concept of capital, from an empirical point of view, it is possible to assume that expropriations, as well as non-free labour, perform an essential role in the accumulation of capital on a global scale (Pradella, 2014; 2017: 155–156).

The assumption that expropriations are part of the capital accumulation is important in understanding in depth the violence of financialisation. As seen, it

From primitive to entangled accumulation 11

is the main characteristic of this advanced stage of capitalism, when the accumulation baseline gives preference to the imperatives of property, increasingly associated with the reproduction of fictitious capital, to the detriment of direct productive revaluation productivity gains. Capitalism thus becomes essentially rentier. Under such conditions, stock owners claim the rent owed to their property and, thereby, appropriate the increasing share of profits drawn from production.

Simultaneously, due to the tendency of capital concentration, capitalists are increasingly becoming investment groups associated with funds and trusts. Withdrawn from productive activities, they await comfortably their gains, taking part of the surplus value created in the economy. If these players delegated the exploitation of wage labour to third parties, they cannot refrain from the production of the surplus that will be appropriated as rent. The result is well known since the 1980s: a decrease in the share of wages in the national income of most countries and attacks on workers' rights.

Financialisation releases capitalists from the drawbacks of productive accumulation: extracting surplus value from living force. Simultaneously, due to the consortium of competing capitals, it needs to enlarge such extraction to remunerate such a large amount of concentrated capital. If something is new now, it must only be the pace and scale of expropriation.

Dispossession, expropriation and the 'rest' of the world

The inside–outside dialectic of capitalist accumulation, which emerges from the combination of postulates developed by Harvey and Dörre, is helpful in understanding the contemporary dynamics of capitalism with a classical yet refurbished lens, especially in the Northern Hemisphere. Still, this dialectic needs to be broadened and complemented in order to grasp different bundles of processes and relations, which have historically confronted capitalism since the colonial period.

As we saw above, for Marx, the point of departure of accumulation implied the need to supply labour-power for the construction of the capitalist system by differentiating between producers and means of production. In addition to this internal capitalist expansion, Marx (2013, 1: 779 ss) refers to the fact that primitive accumulation also depended on external expansion, whose driving force was colonialism. In his words:

> The discovery of gold and silver in America, the extirpation, enslavement and entombment in mines of the aboriginal population, the beginning of the conquest and looting of the East Indies, the turning of Africa into a warren for the commercial hunting of black-skins, signalised the rosy dawn of the era of capitalist production. These idyllic proceedings are the chief momenta of primitive accumulation.
>
> (Marx, 1906 [1867]: 823)

Marx understood that in parallel to the transition from feudalism to wage labour in Western Europe and with the drive towards industrialisation, primitive

12   *From primitive to entangled accumulation*

accumulation gradually shifted from Europe to the colonies. Through colonialism, previously unimaginable spaces opened up for expansion, along with the capitalist annexation of non-capitalist territories which, physically, were many times greater than those first spaces of capitalist expansion in Europe itself. Today, a fierce debate among primitive accumulation theorists is taking place regarding Marx's understanding of the role of colonialism in capitalism as well as the most adequate way of interpreting the place of the colonies in the expansion of accumulation. For some authors, colonialism can be treated as part of the process of accumulation of capital, but not as capitalist accumulation itself given the fact that the aspect that is most distinctive in capitalism (namely, the extraction of surplus value) does not take place in the context of colonialism. For other authors, capitalist accumulation could have indeed taken place in the extraction of surplus value in the colonies as well.[4]

Despite its relevance, this debate seems to miss the essential point, namely, the indisputable interpenetration between the processes of capital accumulation (whether we call it capitalist or not) that occurred within the scope of colonialism and the expansion of industrial capitalism in Europe. As has been abundantly documented, since the pioneering work carried out by Williams (1983 [1944]) at the latest, capital accumulated trough colonial exploitation and slave trade financed not only the construction of libraries, operas and other jewels of the European Enlightenment, but also the development of inventions such as the steam engine (Blackburn, 1988). In many cases, ships fuelled trilateral trade in a single voyage, bringing guns and goods manufactured in British factories to be exchanged for enslaved humans on the African coast, who were then traded for tropical commodities sold in Europe or even processed in the same British factories. In the same way, the one-sided trade agreements with the colonies and even with faltering colonial empires, as was the case of the Treaty of 1810 between Britain and Portugal, established a global division of labour, which guaranteed British industrial accumulation by transferring capital from the colonies and weaker European national economies to Britain.[5]

The inseparability of the processes of accumulation observed in the colonies and in Western Europe was the object of a vast discussion among dependency theorists in the 1970s, particularly in the work of Frank (1978). Frank starts from the notion of *superexploitation*, developed by Marx (1906 [1867]: 654) and taken up by Marini (1967: 129 ff), to refer to the conversion of the minimum required for the worker's subsistence into the foundation of capital accumulation.

For Frank, superexploitation can occur both in the context of wage work and in other relations of production, or, alternatively, in the connection between these two spheres. In the context of wage labour, this implies the payment of a salary below what would be required for the reproduction of the labour-power. In the context of other relations of production, as in the case of slavery or contemporary forms of bonded labour, capital accumulation robs producers of part of their necessary funds for consumption. Ultimately, in the context of the connection between wage and non-salaried work, this means understanding that this pillage taking place in non-capitalist production is directly related to the necessary funds

From primitive to entangled accumulation 13

for consumption and the reproduction of the labour-power of the wage worker, thus constituting an important factor in the creation of extra surplus value (Frank, 1978: 240 ff).

The key issue here is therefore to identify how processes of superexploitation in non-capitalist relations contribute to the capitalist dynamic of accumulation. To do so, Frank (1978: 241) recovers the concept of primitive accumulation, conceptualising it as 'accumulation on the basis of production with non-capitalist relations of production'. For him, primitive accumulation is, in fact, a non-capitalist accumulation of capital. Using this idea as a springboard, Frank differentiates between three types of primitive accumulation: pre-capitalist, non-capitalist contemporary with capitalist accumulation, and postcapitalist. The first corresponds to the 'prehistoric stage of capital' and thus refers to the original accumulation which occurred inside or outside of Europe three or more centuries prior to the Industrial Revolution. According to Frank, this mode of accumulation led to the accrual of a large mass of capital hoarded within pre-capitalist relations of production, including colonialism, slavery and servitude (Frank, 1978: 242–243).

The second type of primitive accumulation is related to the idea of a permanent kind of primitive accumulation which Frank (1978: 243 ff) calls primary accumulation, precisely to distinguish it from pre-capitalist primitive accumulation. It invariably accompanies the capitalist process of accumulation of capital, creating the superexploitation of wage labour by linking the basis of consumption of the latter to a non-capitalist relation of production. Finally, postcapitalist accumulation concerns the socialist economies of the 20th century. According to Frank (1978: 247–248), these also enabled capitalist accumulation by transferring part of the value generated by the labour of planned economies via the trade of goods and raw materials between socialist and capitalist countries, thus guaranteeing profit.

Frank particularly emphasises the roles that pre-capitalist primitive accumulation and primary accumulation have played in the formation and development of capitalist relations of production. Regarding the first, based on Marx's affirmation (1906 [1867]: 833) that 'the veiled slavery of the wage-workers in Europe needed, for its pedestal, slavery pure and simple in the new world', he asserts the idea that the extreme exploitation of non-capitalist social formations in its pre-industrial stage, which materialises in the form of the violent pillage of the consumption funds needed for the reproduction of the worker, is a fundamental precondition for capitalist accumulation. The degree of exhaustion of the workers provoked by this superexploitation can be observed, for example, in '[t]he seven 'useful' years of a slave's life in many parts of the New World, [in] the decline in Indian population in Mexico from 25 million to 1.1 million (and the rise in labour costs for mining) in little more than a century after the Conquest' (Frank, 1978: 243).

Departing from the concept of primary accumulation, Frank affirms that many of these relations of production remained and continue to remain fundamental for the capitalist development of the accumulation of capital. However, it is not simply a matter of acknowledging that they serve as a basis of development.

14   *From primitive to entangled accumulation*

Frank (1978: 244) goes a step further by contending that primary accumulation is a constitutive element of the process of capitalist accumulation, given that the separation of producers in relation to the means of production have contributed to the concentration of capital, thus producing surplus value. Here, once again, the dimension of superexploitation plays a fundamental role as it ensures that non-capitalist relations of production remain impregnated in the development of salaried work itself. Therefore, these persist despite 'the process of divorcing owners from their means of production' (Frank, 1978: 244). How? Through the payment of wage labour at levels lower than what is necessary for the reproduction of the labour-power and for the maintenance of an ever-available reserve army of labour (Frank, 1978: 246).

Hence, Harvey, Dörre and Frank all follow in Luxemburg's footsteps, though each in their own way. However, some contemporary academics like Roberts (2017) have pointed towards a different semantic precursor for the concept of primitive accumulation. They defend Marx in the face of possible insufficiencies suggested by the tradition that takes up Luxemburg's line of thought. For Roberts, Marx clearly identifies expropriations as a perpetual motor of capitalist development, not just as an original moment separating workers from the means of production. In developing research on the notion of expropriation, Fontes (2010; 2017) follows a similar line of argument by seeking in the work of Marx itself the roots for a critique of the reformulated concept of primitive accumulation based on Luxemburg's work.

Fontes argues that Luxemburg's thesis – that capitalist development requires a non-capitalist exterior – may be attentive to certain relevant aspects at the beginning of the 20th century, but it is also problematic. Firstly, it obfuscates the understanding of the *internal* dynamic of capitalist expansion itself as a process that aggravates the conditions of its own social base (Fontes, 2017: 2205 and 2208). Moreover, this difficulty is exacerbated by the fact that the imperialist expansion of capitalism significantly reduced the so-called external borders of accumulation in the course of the 20th century.

For Fontes (2017: 2201 ff), the idea of continued primitive accumulation, particularly the way Harvey reformulates it, runs into at least three problems in the face of such a transformation: (1) the lack of empirical plausibility on account of the creation of a global market and the globalisation of capitalism; (2) dualist reductionism between a normalised capitalism and a predatory capitalism; and (3) the reproduction of a teleology of modernisation which, contained in the conceptual construction of an 'exterior', reproduces a dichotomy between (normalised) capitalist and (primitive) non-capitalist countries. The main problem with this thesis of externality is thus the attribution of a dual character to capitalist accumulation, its result being to imbue a different 'quality' to the (supposed) two forms of accumulation. On the one hand, the broadened (more advanced) economic duress which, though subject to crises, would be based on 'free' workers; on the other hand, the open and archaic violence of primitive accumulation (Fontes, 2017: 2205).

Instead, Fontes (2017: 2202 ff) maintains that the expansion of capitalism never occurred in the form of a fully normalised accumulation, but rather it was

From primitive to entangled accumulation 15

always grounded in speculation, pillage, fraud and blatant theft. Put another way: productive and established accumulation under a legal form of contract between capital and labour was always accompanied by expropriations. This overlap can be seen, for example, in the 'brutal colonisation of Asia towards Industrial Capital in the 19th century [in the coexistence of] the so-called Welfare State 'glorious years' [and] fierce dictatorships imposed throughout the most distant parts of the planet' etc. (Fontes, 2017: 2202). According to Fontes (2017: 2203), fraud and theft are inherent to capitalist expansion, but have historically been practised most frequently and openly in the colonies and post-colonies. Both have only recently become evident for observers of the development of capitalism in the pioneering industrial nations of the Global North, since the most predatory forms of capitalism have now spread to these societies. As the author told her Marxist colleagues from the global North: 'Welcome to real global capitalism as we, in the Global South, have known it since the colonial expansion!'

In order to demonstrate that capitalism has never exhibited a normalised economic form separate from explicit violence, Fontes refers to Volume III of *Capital*, in contrast to the other cited authors who emphasise Chapter 24 of Volume I. She shows that Marx already understood that, once they are generalised, capitalist relations of production are grounded in expropriations.[6] However, Fontes (2010: 44) argues that these expropriations are not the outlet or commodification of a non-capitalist exterior, but the 'expansion of the conditions that exasperate the availability of workers for [the usage of] capital'. Such expansion accompanies the scale of concentration of capital. Thus, at any given historical moment, specific connections develop in which dominant capitalist forces intensify the means by which disparate social situations and populations already incorporated into capitalism in unequal relations are rendered subaltern (Fontes, 2017: 2202).

For Fontes (2010: 44 ff), these multiple expropriations can be placed into two categories: primary and secondary expropriations. The first refers to the loss of the direct ownership of the means of production, mainly land. This is especially true in the case of land taken from peasants in the countryside. Secondary expropriations, on the other hand, refer to the contemporary concentration of capital and materialise in the privatisation of the provision of goods and public services as well as in the suspension of workers' rights. These expropriations may also concern natural resources, such as the conversion of fresh and saltwater, forests, etc. into monopolised property. Yet for Fontes, the most worrisome facet of secondary expropriations is the private appropriation of life itself, both non-human and human, by means of patents and other methods.

By stressing the expropriation of nature, Fontes revisits, albeit implicitly, discussions developed by Marxist feminists starting in the 1970s, who see an important point of reference in the so-called Bielefeld School.[7] The Bielefeld School seeks to offer a theory of repression and exploitation of the so-called 'three colonies' (women, nature and the 'Third World') in capitalist accumulation. In other words: they seek to grasp why violent capitalist oppression is directed at these three spheres as well as which role reproductive work and informal subsistence production play in the development of capitalism (Haubner, 2015: 2).

16 *From primitive to entangled accumulation*

There remains one more fruitful avenue for the contemporary study of phenomena which could easily be classified, using Fontes's categories, as a form of secondary expropriation: profit-making in virtual social networks. Here, expropriation takes place in at least two discrete forms: the sharing economy and the expropriation of the work and data of users.

The most striking feature of large companies such as Uber or Airbnb, which exploit the sharing economy, as an illuminating study by Fairweather (2017) illustrates, is that the extraction of surplus value is possible without the divorce of workers from the means of production. On the contrary, the preservation of property or at least the right to use one's own vehicle to transport passengers or to use real estate leased seasonally is a necessary condition for the driver or the accommodation provider to be able to produce surplus value for the giants Uber and Airbnb. Albeit these firms have equipped offices and employed personnel in the form of a 'conventional wage–labour paradigm' (Fairweather, 2017: 54) and also maintain the control over the software that connects the providers and users of their services, it seems obvious that the lion's share of the surplus these companies appropriate does not stem from their own employees, but rather from the 'autonomous' providers of transport and accommodation.

In the case of companies that sell the data of social network users, search engines and music and video portals such as Google, Facebook and Youtube, the expropriation of 'prod*users*', as Ekman (2012) shows, occurs on various levels. The most obvious is the expropriation, that is, the lack of payment for inherent work or any online activity of the prod*users*, as these activities are monitored and transformed into conglomerates of data about users and preferences, which are then sold to other companies or used as a reference for the allocation of paid advertisements. One could also add all the uninterrupted information in the personal archives and about users' families that are published on platforms such as Facebook or Instagram that the companies monitor, sell or imitate. From the perspective of accumulation, it is also relevant that companies are integrated into virtual personal networks insofar as followers or likes represent not only the possibility for companies to communicate with potential customers in a direct and focused way, but also because likes and followers aggregate value to the wealth of companies and brands (Ekman, 2012).

Both the companies involved in the sharing economy as well as those that transform the information of their online users into commodities have been capable of incorporating an array of activities, resources and social relations previously situated outside the circuit of capitalist accumulation – such as a guest room offered by a family, honeymoon photos or a friend's list of favourite songs – into the dynamic of surplus value production. Although this type of activity is not (yet) economically relevant for the study of accumulation in the port of Rio de Janeiro, it seems important to take note of this form of expropriation for one simple reason. The commercial value that these companies have acquired in a very short period – they are already among the most valuable companies of contemporary capitalism – reinforces, as few other cases do, the plausibility of the theory of capitalist expropriation.

From primitive to entangled accumulation 17

Violence and political-regulatory interventions in capitalist expropriations: bloody legislation and public–private partnerships

As we have just seen, the process of primitive accumulation and the ongoing expropriations can only be brought to fruition by means of non-economic violence, and indeed, it was non-economic violence that was historically exercised by the state with its expropriations and political-regulatory interventions. In the context of colonial Portugal, in addition to the state, the Catholic Church and, more specifically, the brotherhoods, congregations and fraternities played a fundamental role in the process of regulating and restricting access, above all, to the common ownership and use of land. Indeed, the Church guaranteed that even in a scarcely populated country such as Brazil from the 16th to 18th century, non-noble population was kept divorced from what was their most important means of production and subsistence: the land (Fridman, 1999). Correspondingly, during the Portuguese colonial enterprise, the relationship with the Catholic Church operated differently to that which occurred in (internal) primitive accumulation in England where, in the wake of the Anglican reform, the suppression of feudal Catholic properties (such as convents) swept peasant inhabitants off of their lands, causing them to become part of the proletariat (Marx, 1906 [1867], 1: 792 ff). In Brazil, the Catholic Church already participated with the colonial state in the processes of primitive accumulation and was not merely the object of expropriation. We revisit this point below when we discuss the history of the port of Rio de Janeiro.

Yet, before we enter into this, it is necessary to stress that it was and is due to the force and violence of regulatory interventions that external, non-commodified spaces could and can be incorporated into the dynamic of capitalist accumulation.[8] Of course, this aspect is not new to the discussion about primitive accumulation and was already widely developed in the work of Marx (1906 [1867], 1: 786), who emphasised the state's role in promoting expropriation during colonialism, when 'the states of Europe plundered the rest of the world, stealing means of production and labour power on a massive scale' (Roberts, 2017: 12).

Both Harvey (2005: 147) and Dörre (2015: 25), while recognising the pertinence of Marx's affirmations regarding the role played by the state in primitive accumulation, make an important caveat when it comes to understanding accumulation by dispossession and expropriations as a constant in the process of the reproduction of capital. These two authors believe that the regulatory interventions carried out by the state are not necessarily marked by the character of usurpation or brutality and thus do not, at least not integrally, reproduce the characteristics of this original process of separation between workers and the means of production described by Marx. This in and of itself should not come as a surprise, considering that the model of the state Marx knew in the 19th century contrasts with the democratic and – in many cases – welfare state contemporarily observed by Dörre and Harvey. In this context, Dörre (2015: 25) believes that political violence should not only be sought in authoritarian conditions, but in the use of a 'politically motivated precarity' to 'discipline' labourers for precarious work in

18   *From primitive to entangled accumulation*

the new spaces of accumulation. However, one must ask: what does this form of politically motivated precarity consist in? A combination of legislations aimed at social control and commodification and privatisation.

To understand this combination within the area of Marxist political economy requires returning to Marx himself. When laying out his analysis of primitive accumulation, Marx creates a fairly complex picture of different and contradictory uses of state regulation. It is not our goal to reconstruct the entire picture in the present chapter; for our argument, however, what is striking is the emphasis he places on penal law. In the context of the violent usurpation of common property in England, Marx identified two historical-legal phases regarding the regulation of the rights to land. The first stretches from the end of the 15th to the 17th century, when usurpation was practised illegally and against the legislation that was meant to restrain it. The second phase began in the 18th century, the moment when this usurpation became legal and the law itself became 'the instrument of theft' (Marx, 1906 [1867], 1: 796).

Both moments, however, were marked by those elements of penal law that Marx called 'bloody legislation'. These laws operated parallel to the expropriation of the peasantry from their lands. As a result of their expulsion, they began to experience the realm of necessity in a different way at the same time that they became completely 'free' to sell their labour-power to the capitalist, yet they could not be automatically absorbed by the industrial economy. On the one hand, manufacturing did not grow at a rate comparable to the elevated number of expropriated peasants; on the other, these peasants, socialised in other practices, did fit into the newly required patterns of labour and modes of life. There thus formed a mass of people not economically absorbed who needed to 'adapt themselves to the discipline of their new condition' (Marx, 1906 [1867], 1: 806). It is from this perspective that Marx (1906 [1867], 1: 808 s) explained the rise of various bloody legislation in England and France directed against vagrancy and pauperisation starting in the 16th century. In his words,

> [t]hus were the agricultural people, first forcibly expropriated from the soil, driven from their homes, turned into vagabonds, and then whipped, branded, tortured by laws grotesquely terrible, into the discipline necessary for the wage system.

As we have seen, parallel to the internal circuit of accumulation (in Britain and France), Marx stresses the role of colonialism as a complementary although external circuit of accumulation. Accordingly, this external accumulation implies subjugation, plunder, pillage and the enslavement of nations and non-European peoples. Therefore, for Marx, as with the expropriation of peasants in Europe, colonisation implied a high degree of force and political intervention. Penal law, more broadly speaking, fulfilled the role of disciplining the labour-power and taking spaces and goods not yet commodified during the process of primitive accumulation in Europe. In the processes of colonisation, although Marx himself does not explore this aspect in more detail, it is necessary to recognise the

From primitive to entangled accumulation 19

nodal role occupied by international law seeing as it guaranteed the partition of the non-European world among the European colonial powers and sustained the racial classifications that made possible the enslavement of Africans and their descendants (Góngora-Mera, 2017; Knox, 2013).

In the relations between colonies and metropoles, colonial state formed the pillars that sustained the pillage of the colonies and slavery. The regulatory repertoire was vast and spanned from one-sided tax regimes to the prohibition on developing activities in the colonies, which could compete with metropolitan priorities. The latter ranged from the right to property that guaranteed masters the privilege of disposing over the work and body of slaves, to the bloody penal law whose aim was to reprimand flight and slave rebellions (Souza, 1999).[9]

In the debates of the last decades on privatisation, other relevant legal instruments have been given prominence for capitalist expropriations, which are closely linked to the role of state regulation in the current regime of financial accumulation. In its present form, all of the actions orientated towards privatising the market of goods and services hitherto produced by the state were developed by means of regulatory interventions and legal reforms. These mechanisms enabled expropriation by means of privatisations and, at the same time, created a precarised mass of individuals by modifying labour laws (the augmented outsourcing of labour, 'flexibilisation' of contracts for temporary labour, etc.) (Dörre, 2015: 42–51). Effectively, incorporating sectors dedicated to the production of goods that, until the 1980s, were in the hands of the state into the dynamic of private accumulation demanded the creation of a comprehensive institutional architecture and new regulatory instruments – with emphasis, as Harvey highlighted (1989: 7), on public–private partnerships.

Public–private partnerships are contracts between the public administration and private groups in which the latter provide, by means of remunerated consideration, infrastructure, services and urban equipment. For Harvey (1989: 7–8), these partnerships are the central characteristic of the new social model of enterprise. They remodelled the previously existing conditions of accumulation that had served as barriers to capitalist expansion. If during the Fordist period, as Harvey (1989: 7) contends, the prevailing model of stewardship was based on the transferral of resources and the direct involvement of public actors in productive activities and investments, the macro-institutional transformations initiated in the 1970s constructed a new economic environment, which became dependent upon the direct negotiation of the financial market and reconstruction of a physical and social landscape that would enable competition for resources and jobs. This was made possible by public–private partnerships. Originating in the objective to transform the landscape by orientating it towards the market, public–private partnerships became the means to the instrumentalisation of space within financialised capitalist accumulation as it has been recently observed in the provision of infrastructure for mega-events such as the Olympic games and world cups (Branski et al., 2013). In other words, public–private partnerships have emerged as essential for pillage, dispossession and usurpations that temporally and spatially readjust the necessary conditions towards the accumulation of finance capital.

20 *From primitive to entangled accumulation*

Given that in the phenomena of expropriation observed by Marx, penal law played the central role in ensuring the separation between producers and the means of production, the restructuring of spaces towards accumulation now also depends on the reconfiguration of other regulatory spheres. In addition to civil law and specific legislation concerning public–private partnerships, the adjustment of urban law and the laws governing the use and occupation of the ground are also relevant as they redefine conducts and uses accepted and punishable in a given urban or rural area.

Theoretically, public–private partnerships can come into being in complete observance of standing laws, i.e. without having to generate any illicit advantages, whether economic or of any other nature, for the parties involved in such negotiations. Nevertheless, the recurrence of corruption scandals involving public–private partnerships forces us to acknowledge that the execution of these partnerships creates an environment that is particularly favourable to the illicit sale of decisions, given the degree of articulation between political decisions and economic advantages. Corruption, understood as an unlawful purchase or sale of political decisions or actions by state actors, thus appears to be part of a systematic mechanism accompanying a dynamic of expropriation carried out in non-commodified spaces (in the case of state resources) to facilitate the expansion of circuits producing surplus value. By way of example, when a building company bribes a minister in order to win an overpriced contract, the former is at the same time expropriating the state and creating conditions to exploit surplus value in the sphere of services sold to the state via the contract that was obtained unlawfully.

Besides the political-regulatory, one last important aspect of contemporary processes of expropriation (which could be contemplated in a historical review and has not yet been adequately explored in the works of Harvey and Dörre) is their linguistic-discursive dimension, as the timely study by Backhouse (2015) shows. When studying so-called 'green grabbing' (*grüne Landnahme*), enabled by the introduction of environmental protection legislation in the state of Pará in Brazilian Amazonia, the author shows that the construction of the rhetorical figure of 'degraded land' – derived from deforestation – was fundamental for the transferral of land belonging to small rural producers to concerns such as the giant mining company Vale. Accordingly, after promoting the eviction of small landholders from areas already deforested, concerns successfully applied for subsidised credits and fiscal advantages offered by the Brazilian government to companies which transform this allegedly 'degraded areas' into palm oil plantations. The argument used for justifying the subsidies is the assumed sustainable character of palm oil as a renewable source of energy, an assumption which has proved to be fallacious (Backhouse et al., 2016).

Entangled accumulation

In order to encompass different developments in the Marxist discussion of primitive accumulation and expropriation as constructed above, we have coined the term 'entangled accumulation'. The expression was inspired by the idea of

From primitive to entangled accumulation   21

entangled modernity, coined by Conrad and Randeria (2002), and its incorporation into the study of global social inequalities under the concept of entangled inequalities (Costa, 2013).

The concept of entangled modernities expresses the fact that, despite being represented in a separate and isolated way in national historiographies, modernity has been global from the time of its very origin seeing as it links and entangles the different regions of the world. In the notion of entangled inequalities, at least three levels of interpenetration and interdependence of social inequalities can be highlighted, namely that: (i) social inequalities found in different regions of the world are always interrelated; (ii) inequalities observed in different historical periods are, necessarily, interconnected; and (iii) inequalities, expressed by means of different systems of stratification (class, race and gender), condition each other (Jelin et al., 2017).

Similarly, entangled capitalist accumulation implies interconnection and interpenetration not only of different regions of the world, but also of different historical periods and even dimensions of capitalist expansion. To systematise this, though by no means exhaustively, we identify at least five levels of interpenetrations inherent to entangled accumulation:

i) The incorporation of new non-commodified spaces into the process of accumulation – as much as these spaces seem to be local – always reflects global dynamics, characterising what Luxemburg (2003 [1913]: 331–334) qualified as the disappearance of the local. This does not imply the complete absorption of the dynamics inside and outside of the process of accumulation observed in the local sphere into one single global dynamic. Though related and interrelated, the multiple scales of accumulation exhibit dynamics of disconnecting and integrating new spaces into the accumulation process with some degree of autonomy. As we describe in detail in the next chapters, this implies that, in certain moments of history, the transformations that have taken place in the port of Rio de Janeiro and its surroundings were completely interdependent with the global capitalist dynamic. This was the case in the periods in which the port functioned as a market for slaves and a port of embarkment for sugar, gold and later coffee. When, starting in the last decades of the 19th century, the port no longer performed these functions, the port district was to a large extent disconnected from the global dynamic of accumulation. Despite constituting an exterior space for global accumulation, urban reforms did seek, with some success, to reintegrate the area into the local dynamic of accumulation. It is true that these reforms exhibit links with Europe and the rest of the world, be it for their inspiration and conception or the financing that was obtained to carry them out. Nevertheless, the inside–outside dynamics of accumulation induced by the reforms have been of predominantly local reach.

ii) None of the various patterns of accumulation described up to now – neither the historical divorce of workers and means of production which Marx referred to, nor the accumulation by dispossession described by Harvey,

22   *From primitive to entangled accumulation*

the financial expropriation described by Dörre, the superexploitation in the terms formulated by Frank, nor the secondary expropriations or expropriation of nature and life underscored by Fontes – have a rigid or fixed chronology, nor are they historically exclusive. That is, these different forms of accumulation can coexist in a single period and in a single geographical space. One form of accumulation can also re-emerge after having disappeared in a preceding phase.

iii) Stemming from this, discrete mechanisms associated with capitalist accumulation, including the mobilisation of law, the state and politics, culture and corruption as well as discursive production as elucidated by Backhouse, also coexist spatially and temporally.

iv) While requiring the intervention of the state, capitalist accumulation, seen from a global perspective and not simply within a particular nation-state, tends to erase the borders between state and market, and even legality and illegality. This can be verified very clearly by looking at the systematic and recurring cases of favouritism and corruption that accompany the public concession of services, processes of privatisation and even the formulation of laws and public policies for the different economic sectors. Even the actions of governments in favour of national companies in the area of foreign policy and their operation in multilateral organs such as the WTO indicate the fluidity of the borders between state and private companies with regard to capitalist accumulation.

v) In the course of the various cycles of accumulation, social categorisations relative to class, gender, ethnicity and race have been interpenetrated, so that socioeconomic hierarchies take on a form which more and more resembles that of entangled inequalities as described above. In the case of the transformations observable in the port district, for example, it appears that from the very moment of arrival and commercialisation of the first contingents of people kidnapped and trafficked from the African coast to the port of Rio de Janeiro, racial classifications and legal status (slave/non-slave) have constituted the most visible hierarchy in that space. Of course, hierarchies of class and gender were present as well and could be compounded with differences between free men, mere service providers and owners of goods and slaves, or with the complete absence of free women, confined as they were to their homes. However, before the advent of slavery, these different hierarchical orders had their own sphere and, to a large extent, independence of action. With the diversification of the regimes of labour in the slave-based society and, with even more emphasis, after the abolition of slavery, these orders interpenetrated one another. As a result, the positions assumed by a given person in the social structure are always a result of the interpenetration of social hierarchies of gender, race, ethnicity, class, etc.

As seen thus far, entangled accumulation has not just been based on the taking of pre-existing physical settings, for this would imply its exhaustion once the geographic expansion of capitalism around the entire world was completed. What we

From primitive to entangled accumulation 23

do see is rather capitalism's permanent capacity to produce new capitalist spaces whenever accumulation encounters a barrier to its expansion. The production of new spaces of accumulation has in this a concrete and specific meaning. It refers to the complete reconfiguration of the physical, legal and social characteristics of the already-occupied setting according to variations in the types of technology, capital and labour-power employed there. It is here that previous relations, forms and patterns of production, consumption, regulation, culture and life are modified by diverse phenomena, including new buildings, urban designs, migratory flows and rules of organisation and control that can maintain or introduce asymmetries and socio-spatial discontinuities.

Notes

1 A previous and slightly different version of this chapter was published in: *European Journal of Social Theory*, online first, January 2019. https://doi.org/10.1177/136843 1018825064

2 The German term *Landnahme* literally means 'land grabbing'. Its theoretical origin was coined by Luxemburg, who recognised the logical nexus between capitalist expansion and the colonial exploitation of non-European countries. As applied by Dörre, this notion takes on a broader meaning: it is the invasion, seizure and occupation of a space or social sphere for the exploitation of all its commodification potential. Importantly, the concept of *Landnahme* cannot be reduced to the English expression land grabbing, which is widespread in the contemporary debate and has a precise technical meaning: the legal or illegal acquisition of large portions of land by transnational companies, foreign governments or private persons to produce food, biofuels or for speculation on a high scale (Borras et al., 2012). The range and theoretical purpose of the term *Landnahme* are much greater. It is a macrosociological concept, that is, it reflects different processes of expropriation of a social space in a broader sense. Thus, it not only refers to geographical territory, but also the incorporation of social relations with the aim of integrating them into capitalist accumulation.

3 For an overview on the broad debate on financialisation and capital accumulation see, among others, Chesnais, 2016; Fine, 2010; Lapavitsas, 2014; and Lavinas, 2017.

4 For a review of the debate, see Roberts, 2017.

5 The 1810 Strangford Treaty between England and Portugal, ratified at a moment when Portugal was being thrashed by the Napoleonic Wars, guaranteed unprecedented tariff advantages for English products to enter Portuguese metropolitan and colonial territories without a corresponding English reciprocity for products from Portugal and its colonies. Virtually, a market reserve was created for English industrial products bought with revenues obtained from the sale of slaves and commodities produced by slaves in the colonies (Caldeira, 2011: 186 ff).

6 For Fontes (2010: 22 ff), the contemporary processes of financialisation of capitalism throw capitalist expropriation in stark relief, as loans accelerate the extraction of surplus value to remunerate both the industrial capitalist and the service provider, not to mention the shareholder. Fontes's thesis, while plausible, does not seem to consider important dimensions of financialisation, such as the indebtedness of both individuals and families, forms of financial rent by manipulating profit expectations instead of charging interest and the role of hedge funds, among others. For this reason, we orient our analysis especially towards the logic of financialisation and dispossession in the terms described by Harvey and summarised above.

7 The Bielefeld School, also called the *Subsistenzansatz* (subsistence approach), was a theoretical movement of feminist and Marxist inspiration, which emerged towards the end of the 1970s and spread widely in the 1980s. Among its main proponents

24   *From primitive to entangled accumulation*

are Maria Mies, Veronika Bennholdt-Thomsen and Claudia von Werlhof. Even though other Marxist-feminist perspectives existed and are even more widespread in the current debate (for instance, the theory of social reproduction), we make reference to the Bielefeld School here because of their dialogue and direct reference to Luxemburg's theory of ongoing primitive accumulation. For a panorama of the Bielefeld School, see Haubner (2015).

8 For a discussion about legal regulation and capitalist expropriation, see Gonçalves 2017; 2018.

9 The role of the state in colonial exploitation was of course not limited to regulation. The state was, in many cases, the co-founder and financer of the colonial enterprise, as Roberts (2017: 12) reminds us in his review of Marx's works: 'Colonial expeditions and commercial wars were financed by the selling of public bonds'.

2 Port, capital and the capital city

In classical geographic models, the interrelations of ports and urban settlements are generally described using the notion of symbiotic trajectory, according to which a reciprocal fertilisation takes place, meaning that ports function as a factor of attraction and influence in the urban system (Ducruet, 2006: 2–3; Bird, 1957: 178 ss). This literature departs from the thesis that maritime commerce has given rise to a series of settlements – for various reasons. On the one hand, commerce depends on the flourishing of companies and jobs needed for the commercial flow of goods, including activities relating to the physical management of loads and the businesses of expedition, finance, insurance, dispatch, etc., and also the construction and technical maintenance of ships (Witherick, 1981; Hilling, 1988). On the other, the movement of loads attracts producers and consumers to the surroundings of the ports.

Yet the notion of the 'port-city symbiotic trajectory' is not capable of explaining dysfunctions that arise out of the relations between the port and the city. For this, we must turn to a critique by Norcliffe, Basset and Hoare (1996: 124), who consider the notion an expression of 'geographical common sense', according to which ports are celebrated as the motor of settlements based on productive sectors, which stimulate the growth of a prosperous urban culture as well as opportunities in terms of wealth and lifestyles offered by commerce. Against this common sense, contemporary geography argues that, in the phase of the 'symbiotic trajectory', there already exist points of decoupling or disjuncture between the port and the city (Ducruet, 2006: 4). Being based on 'dirty' and 'dangerous' forms of business from the social and environmental points of view, the productive port sectors make way for housing for stevedores and spaces of entertainment for sailors and navigators, thus rendering them a less valued part of the land and of the urban fabric. Accordingly, commercial classes and other sectors of the local elites tend to live and work far away from the port district, not only generating a physical divorce from the city, but converting the areas of the port into a social, aesthetic and political world apart (Norcliffe et al., 1996: 125).

Using the logic of entangled accumulation as a springboard, it is possible to reinterpret these points of divorce or disjuncture as tendencies to decouple a space from the dynamic of value production. These movements are necessary for the construction of a new 'exterior', which, in turn, is essential to maintain

26 *Port, capital and the capital city*

accumulation. Accordingly, this new 'exterior' can be conceptualised as a new non-commodified space which gives rise to a new dynamic of reincorporation into the process of accumulation.

In this way, without neglecting the contributions made by critical contemporary geography to the notion of the 'port-city symbiotic trajectory', we understand the integration between the development of the port and the city based on the inherent contradictions to every process of capital accumulation.

To discuss entangled accumulation in the context of the port district of Rio de Janeiro, we depart from three different ways in which the port is inserted into the capitalist dynamic. Firstly, the port is considered in its *functions-end*, i.e. it permits the entry and departure of wares and persons in and out of the city and the country. Since the colonial period, this flow of goods has ensured Brazilian integration into the global dynamic of accumulation. Secondly, we examine how accumulation occurs in the space of the port itself. Here, we look at the port's *activity-means*, i.e. the generation of value by means of services offered upon the embarkment, disembarkment and storage of wares. Lastly, we deal with the *interaction* which takes place between the port, its vicinity and the whole of the city. In this web of relations, the occupation and construction of the physical space of the port district itself is inserted into the inside–outside–within dynamics of capitalist accumulation. These three modes of integration of the port district into the dynamic of accumulation have varied over time, and with them, the prevalent forms of incorporation of non-commodified spaces have varied in each period, too.

A brief historical–spatial panorama of the port and the city of Rio de Janeiro

It is not easy to pinpoint the exact date that marks the birth of a port in Rio de Janeiro. In January 1502, less than two years after the first disembarkation of the Portuguese from the coast of what is today the state of Bahia, located many hundreds of kilometres to the north of Rio de Janeiro, the Portuguese Navigator Gaspar de Lemos 'discovered' the bay where, in 1565, the first settlement created by the Jesuits would be founded at the foot of the famous Sugarloaf Mountain. Lemos believed that the bay was the mouth of a river, hence the name (*rio* means river in Portuguese) that the city bears to today. Before they installed themselves in the region, the Portuguese had to ally themselves with the indigenous Temininós to defeat the French who, allied with the Confederation of the Tamoios, a league of indigenous peoples who resisted Portuguese colonisation, controlled the bay from the fort they had erected on the Island of Sergipe (Williams et al., 2016: 9 ss).

A permanent and stable Portuguese settlement was only made possible by the occupation and construction of a small fortified city on the Hill of Castelo, beginning in 1567, in the region which today corresponds to the centre of Rio de Janeiro. After occupying the Hill of Castelo, the lower parts were occupied between the hills of São Bento, Santo Antônio and Conceição in order to construct an urban centre there; this took place already towards the end of the 16th century (Fridman, 1999: 88).

Port, capital and the capital city 27

It is precisely at the 'bottom of the Hill of Castelo (today Street of Misericórdia), where anchorage was favourable', that the regular port activities commenced, which had already taken on significance in the first decades of the 17th century (Lamarão, 1991: 22), when anchoring in that port was restricted to embarkations of lesser draught. Cargo and persons transported by vessels across the Atlantic were docked in the ocean to avoid running aground in the shallow waters close to the port. They were subsequently re-embarked in smaller vessels and transported from there to the port. The construction of a larger wharf would only be carried out after the arrival of the Portuguese royal family in 1808. Despite the existing limitations, from the end of the 17th century, Rio de Janeiro began consolidating itself with its port activities as a fundamental nucleus of global commercial networks:

> Yet colonial Rio emerged as a global city, linked to Europe, Asia, and Africa, through the circulation of people, goods, and ideas that travelled by ship. The city served as entrepôt for a range of commodities – wines and cane brandies, commercialised foodstuffs, precious metals and gemstones, valuable spices, and enslaved labourers – coveted in regional and global markets.
>
> (Williams et al., 2016: 12)

Historically, the first function performed by the port was to integrate Brazil as a Portuguese colony into the global economy. To some extent, the port functioned as the nexus that linked the space of primitive accumulation to the future epicentre of capitalism in Europe. That is, the port originated in the interests of the Portuguese coloniser firstly in draining the land of its redwood and sugar, and later the gold which was plundered in Minas Gerais beginning in the first years of the 18th century. The port was equally important as an entrepôt in the commerce of goods and slaves and served a key function in the connection with the port of Buenos Aires, thus inscribing itself into the commercial routes that linked Europe, Africa and the Spanish and Portuguese colonial realms in the Americas. Also important was the port's function in establishing the link with the backcountry of the Brazilian colony, from where exported sugar and wood were brought via waterways and rudimentary roads in the first centuries of the Portuguese colonisation of Brazil. Lastly, the port served as a place to store rare goods arriving from the metropolis and to embark primary products stemming from agriculture or mining (Figueiredo, 2005: 24–25, see also Soares and Moreira, 2007: 104; Honorato, 2008: 31; Moura, 1995: 64 and Tavares, 2012: 48 ss).

The growing importance of Rio de Janeiro and its port in colonial geopolitics led to the city being declared the capital post of the Brazilian colony in 1763, thus superseding the city of Salvador, the first capital of the colony. It is worth highlighting the role of the Catholic Church in occupying the region around the first location of the port near the Hill of Castelo – and not only there, but in all of the city in its first centuries of existence. At that time, the religious orders and confraternities were the large landowners by definition. The Church constructed and leased housing and controlled the hospitals, pharmacies; it also supplied

28   *Port, capital and the capital city*

the settlement with food produced in its gardens and mills (Fridman, 1999: 14). Further, insofar as the existing hierarchies between the different religious brotherhoods were associated with existing social hierarchies in local societies, the social occupation and use of the urban space followed the logic of segmentation and segregation already in the first centuries of the city's existence, as Fridman's sound analysis shows (1999: 49):

> [E]ach order or confraternity controlled a parcel of territory. Those that gathered the wealthiest were in the *heart* of the city and were served by colleges, hospitals, the port, the fountains, the drainage of rainwater, the markets or symbolic landmarks such as churches, cemeteries or procession routes. The poorest brotherhoods established themselves in the Rossio, which, because of its location, represented a new banishment for them. They were the reflection and condition of the existing division in society as a whole, discriminatory to the point that there existed brotherhoods for browns, mulattos, blacks and unassimilated whites. As such, properties represented a mechanism by which the space of the city which was taking shape came to be differentiated as a consequence of the social practices carried out within it.

The port and the city of Rio de Janeiro became even more relevant when the Portuguese Crown, seeking refuge from Napoleonic expansion in Europe, moved to Brazil in 1808 and brought along a significant body of bureaucrats, artists and intellectuals.[1] In the same period, the Crown also decided to open Brazilian ports to ships from 'friendly nations', abolishing the hitherto existing legislation which restricted access to Portuguese ships.

Since the second half of the 18th century, the most important activities linked to the slave trade were being transferred from the centre to the port, where the Valongo Complex was installed. It was comprised of a lazarette, a cemetery and a slave market, establishments dedicated to the preparation of slaves for public exposition and sale. This preparation included fattening them up and applying whale oil to their skin. They were even administered stimulants to hide from buyers the sicknesses, sores, and trauma and apathy they experienced in their abduction from Africa and the transatlantic crossing. All of this was registered in many travel logs and reports written by Europeans who visited the port in the period.[2] In 1843, the port was completely remodelled and in part banked by direct order of the Brazilian Emperor Peter II to receive 'the princess of the Two Sicilies, Teresa Cristina Maria of Bourbon, whom he had married by proxy and who was arriving from Italy to become the Empress of Brazil' (Lima et al., 2016: 300–301).

It is true that the definitive prohibition of the slave trade in 1850 – which, as slavery itself, had survived the independence of Brazil in 1822 – stripped the port of one of its fundamental functions. Even so, the simultaneous expansion of international trade and the continued growth in the export of coffee from the Paraíba Valley maintained the vitality of the port activities.

The prohibition of the slave trade and the absorption of the remaining slaves into the coffee plantations were accompanied by the diffusion of relations of

Port, capital and the capital city 29

wage work in Rio de Janeiro, a city which was 'being transfigured more and more by the new framework of social relations that were forming in the urban space' (Benchimol, 1992: 44). In fact, the capital of the Empire exhibited a complex social structure in the last decades of the 19th century. According to the census of 1870, this social structure encompassed a total urban population of 192,002 inhabitants (235,381 inhabitants if also including rural parishes), a majority of whom were free men (81% of the total). Close to one-third of the total population was made up of foreigners (Benchimol, 1992: 79).

In the second half of the 19th century, urban transportation played a fundamental role in structuring the urban layout of Rio de Janeiro. Run by private enterprises 'operating in an area of privilege conceded by the state', horse-drawn tram lines departed from the centre to the residential neighbourhoods in the northern and southern parts of town, connecting the residential areas, especially the somewhat more removed population, and the 'hectic, multifaceted, overcrowded and unhealthy area' dominated by tenement houses inhabited by the poor and destitute (Benchimol, 1992: 96).

The abolition of slavery in 1888, the proclamation of the Republic in 1889 and the simultaneous decline in the cultivation of coffee in the Paraíba Valley were accompanied by important changes in Rio de Janeiro. Between 1870 and 1890, the population of the city doubled, jumping to 522,651 inhabitants, 24% of whom were foreigners. Various factories emerged in the federal capital, producing consumer goods such as fabrics, food and footwear for the rapidly expanding internal market (Benchimol, 1992: 172–174).

The new inhabitants of the city included an important body of persons who had come from the former capital of the colony, Salvador, the majority of whom were ex-slaves:

> Upon arrival in Rio, they established themselves first in Saúde, the old Valongo, where housing was inexpensive, and the port offered the opportunity of manual labour. They commonly had a well-defined identity: Blacks of Sudanese origin, they brought with them from Salvador wide experience, both cultural, stemming from their participation in festive groups, and religious, related to the *Candomblé* religion.
>
> (Figueiredo, 2005: 185)

This is the general context in which the various urban and port reform projects took place at the turn of the 20th century. What is particularly representative here are the works launched by Rodrigues Alves, who became president of Brazil in 1902. Contrary to his nickname, the 'Snooze', Rodrigues Alves dedicated himself with fervour to the task of modernising the federal capital. He broadened the circulation plan in the central district and promoted a wide reform of the port. The works were financed via a tremendous loan from the Rothschild family (one of the most famous dynasties of European banking families) as well as national capital 'gained by means of passing special policies' (Figueiredo, 2005: 175). The cycle of urban modernisation in the initial years

30 *Port, capital and the capital city*

of the 20th century was completed by the actions of mayor Pereira Passos, who governed the city between 1902 and 1906.

In its *activity-end*, that is, in permitting the entry and exit of wares, the port remained relevant until the Second World War, when it ceded its importance to other Brazilian ports. From then on, the port district lost its relevance for the accumulation of capital in all of the three areas highlighted here: as a chain link between the Brazilian economy and the global economy, as a space of value production for the provision of port services and as a physical space for urban expansion. Consequently, the real estate in the area, though geographically central, had little value for the market. Compared to the more and more valuable area expanding along the coast towards the south as well as the new business opportunities arising with the increasing population density of the suburbs in the north, the port district was a territory of little interest for investments and capitalist accumulation. Also relevant in this process was the expansion of the roads in the city centre, whose climax was the 1944 inauguration of the avenue idealised by then Brazilian dictator Getúlio Vargas and christened with his name. Significantly, with the construction of Avenida Presidente Vargas, the port district was 'cut off from the city's beating heart by a 16-lane expressway that was difficult to cross' (Cardoso, 2015: 188).[3]

With the move of the federal capital to Brasília in 1960 and the subsequent political and economic depletion of Rio de Janeiro, the abandonment of the port district simply worsened; it received none of the large investments in infrastructure and urban renewal directed towards other parts of the city during the military dictatorship between 1964 and 1985. It is interesting to note that, together with the Perimetral Bridge, which was constructed in 1950 and allowed vehicles to travel around the area on an elevated bridge, other road projects in the port district and its surroundings devalued this urban area even more. They all aimed to link strategic poles from the economic and political points of view, specifically, the centre-south area and the new international airport created in 1952, the exits for neighbouring states, the link between the north, where the bulk of the working-class population lived, and their workplaces and service providers in the south. In these connections, the port district was a mere transit route, a passage emptied of any meaning and content for those who wanted to arrive as quickly as possible at their destination.

This picture only began to change in the 1980s, when the Commercial Association of Rio de Janeiro proposed to demolish various buildings in the district in order to construct a commercial centre, taking advantage of the possibilities of embarkment and disembarkment offered by the port. This can clearly be seen as an attempt at entangled accumulation in the sense described above insofar as it was sought to incorporate a space weakly integrated into the dynamic of accumulation by recapturing the dynamism of capitalist development in Rio de Janeiro. The project clashed with the local population, who organised to ensure that 1100 buildings in the port district were recognised as historical heritage, as shown by Vassallo's meticulous reconstruction (2015: 64). What is more, the intent of the Commercial Association to modify how the area was occupied can

Port, capital and the capital city 31

be added to other proposals which arose in the same period, all of which ended in frustration, according to Andreatta and Herce (2011) because 'they were not very realistic, seeing as they had not been previously negotiated, neither with the owner of the port (the Federal Government did) nor with concessionary operator (Docas-Rio)'.

The plans of urban reform were taken up again by the mayors César Maia (1993–1996 and 2001–2008) and Luís Paulo Conde (1997–2000), who began to modify legislation governing the use and occupation of the urban terrain to create the legal conditions for the desired interventions in the port district. Yet it was during the administration of Eduardo Paes (2009–2016), as we will show below, that the most relevant legal and institutional alterations to enable a wide urban reform in the district were carried out, with the purpose of reintegrating the areas contiguous to the port into capitalist accumulation.

The changes in the physical location of the port activities of Rio de Janeiro demand some clarification. Between the end of the 18th century and the beginning of the 19th century, the port activities (which had taken place next to the coastal strip close to the Hill of São Bento in the beginning of the 16th century) were transferred to the Valongo Wharf, located more to the north in the area where, today, the neighbourhoods of Saúde and Gamboa are situated. At the end of the 20th century, the activities shifted even more to the north, to the district of Caju (Cardoso, 2015: 188). It should also be emphasised that, until stricter regulation took effect in the 17th century, discrete spots on the coastal strip close to the urban nucleus installed within the bay were used for anchorage, especially for lesser embarkations. Equally important for the flow of the production coming from the interior were the fluvial ports situated near the mouths of the 33 rivers, which drained into the Bay of Guanabara (Fridman, 1999: 87).

Strictly speaking, one would have to study the dynamics of connection, disconnection and reconnection to capitalist accumulation in each of the districts contiguous to the different locations of the port activities. Yet the transformations observed in the Hill of Castelo after the port was transferred to the Valongo Wharf are particularly representative of capitalist accumulation. Already in the second half of the 19th century, there were calls to simply demolish the Hill of Castelo with the justification that the old stately houses had transformed into degraded tenement houses and it was necessary to remove the 'prostitutes, laundresses and *Candomblé* priests' and 'incorporate this territory of the city under a new order' (Silva, 2003: 47). For this purpose, in 1891, the then influential entrepreneur Carlos Sampaio created in 1891 the 'Company for the Removal of the Hill of Castelo'. Many opposed this, believing it was possible to recover and re-urbanise the area without removal. Finally, in 1922, in the context of the celebrations of the centennial of Brazilian independence, the former entrepreneur Carlos Sampaio, who had meanwhile managed to become the mayor of Rio de Janeiro, carried out the removal of the Morro, transporting the land to flooded areas and for land reclamation works.

Despite the illustrative character of the Hill of Castelo and the transformations in the area of the port after it was transferred to the district of Valongo and

32 *Port, capital and the capital city*

Prainha, the history of these transformations lies beyond the scope of this book. We thus limit ourselves to briefly mentioning the disputes in the surroundings of the first port situated near the Hill of Castelo until the end of the 18th century, when it was the main port of the city. From there, we shift our attention to the area contiguous to the second location of the port, in the area of Prainha and Valongo, where the port activities were developed from the end of the 18th century towards the end of the 20th century. It is in this area charged with historical and cultural references that the most recent project of urban renewal, Porto Maravilha, takes place. To analyse this project, we are particularly interested in the transformations observed in the rectangular area delimited by the Avenida Francisco Bicalho, Avenida Presidente Vargas, Avenida Rio Branco and the coastal strip, made up of the neighbourhoods of Saúde, Santo Cristo and the area bordering on Cidade Nova, including the hills of Providência, Pinto and Gamboa.

The transformations around the neighbourhood of Caju, to which the port activities were transferred at the end of the 20th century, are not contemplated here.

Final remarks

The economic activity of the port of Rio de Janeiro was fundamental for the inclusion of Brazil in the regime of global accumulation. According to Luxemburg (2013 [1913]: 331–334), the expansion of capitalist accumulation demands the incorporation of spaces that do not yet produce in the capitalist sense, in this case, colonies in Latin America, the Caribbean, Asia and Africa. On the one hand, the dynamisation of Rio's port allowed the absorption of consumer goods, such as fabrics and European manufactured goods in Brazil, and even articles such as porcelain and adornments, in particular from India and China. In the following period, other European-made goods used in production, for example in the construction of railways, entered Brazil via the port. On the other hand, the port served as an exit for metals and precious minerals and commodities produced in the colony, including sugar, coffee, rice and tropical woods (Fridman, 1999: 107). From this perspective, the economic role played by the port should be placed in the context of the maritime technological revolution and the permanent diminution of the costs of transport beginning in the 18th century, which according to O'Rourke and Williamson (1999: 33) fostered the consolidation of an integrated commodity market within the Atlantic economy.

As a hub for the entry and exit of products, the port needed to be efficient. Hence, the permanent demand for the improvement of its installations was instrumental if the port was to function as one of the central links in the chain that articulated accumulation in the Americas, Africa and Europe. To translate these processes into Marxist terms (see Luxemburg, 2003 [1913]: 300–302), the port promoted imports of consumer goods from Europe. Thereby, consumption of consumer goods by social groups in Brazil who were not yet directly integrated into the circuit of accumulation propelled the European consumer goods industry (Sector 2) as well as the European producer goods industry (Sector 1),

Port, capital and the capital city 33

which sold machines necessary for the expansion of Sector 2. With this, it heated the economy and the consumer market of the respective European country, creating more productive capacity and work possibilities in both Sector 1 and Sector 2.

Equally significant for this colonial expansion of capitalism was the trafficking of slaves from Africa to the Americas and, to a lesser extent, to Europe. As we will show, trading slaves for manufactured wares from Europe, such as textiles and arms in African ports, in addition to other commodities originating from the Americas and Asia, permitted the expansion of the production of consumer goods and production goods (machines) in Europe, in addition to augmenting the accumulation of mercantile capital and the resulting offer of capital for investment in the nascent European industry.

In this context, extensive and dynamic port zones (such as that of Rio de Janeiro) in colonial non-capitalist territories became an alternative and a necessity in the expansion process of global capital, given that accumulation there did not fundamentally occur by extracting surplus value. The entangled character of the accumulation observed here is self-evident inasmuch as established economic relations promoted the interpenetration of capitalist and non-capitalist spaces in different regions of the world, as well as the co-creation of different patterns of accumulation: primary and secondary expropriations, accumulation by dispossession and by creating surplus, as well as mercantile, industrial and financial accumulation.

In the following three chapters, we will show in a more detailed manner how different processes of expropriation and forms of accumulation have been entangled in the space of the port in four different historical phases: (1) the predominance of the mercantile–slave economy, (2) the expansion of industrial capitalist accumulation, (3) the current process of financialisation and (4) the contemporary economic, political and social crises.

Notes

1 Incidentally, the idea of transferring the capital of the Portuguese colonial empire to Brazil had been circulating in Portugal since the late 16th century, as Gerstenberger (2015:38) explains:

> 'In fact, the idea of moving the Portuguese capital to the New World of America in order to achieve a better geopolitical foothold already emerged in the late 16th century when Portugal was annexed by Castile (the Iberian 'Union' lasted sixty years from 1580 to 1640). Since then, clerics and politicians repeatedly recommended the establishment of the capital of the Portuguese Empire in the New World'.

2 For an overview, see Schwarcz (2017).
3 The case of Avenida Presidente Vargas (which, instead of integrating, separates the various zones of the city) is one of many disastrous urban interventions – and reactions to these interventions – the city of Rio de Janeiro has seen. Cardoso (2015: 188) hits the nail on the head when he states that: 'In the history of Rio de Janeiro, the best intentions of successive governments have paved the road to hell, and the best way to escape redevelopment has been to stay invisible'.

3 Capitalism and slavery in the port of Rio de Janeiro

From the first uses of the area as a dock in the 16th century until the end of the 19th century, the port took part in classical patterns of primitive accumulation. It integrated Brazil into world capitalism through the export of primary products, the import of manufactured goods and the trade of hundreds of thousands of enslaved Africans. Indeed, this port received the highest number of enslaved Africans of the entire American continent, making it the largest market for slaves the world has ever known. During the 18th century alone, close to 850,000 enslaved persons landed at the port of Rio de Janeiro; in the following century, around 700,000 persons did so. Apart from satisfying the consumption needs of the city and plantations in the region, the port functioned as a warehouse for humans to be resold in the remaining provinces of the Southeast and South of Brazil (Florentino, 2014: 43, 50; Lima et al., 2016: 309).

The search for explanations for the fact that the Portuguese coloniser 'opted' for slavery has long mobilised the attention of Brazilian historians and political economists, from Caio Prado Júnior (1986 [1945]) to Celso Furtado (1967 [1959]), Maria Sylvia de Carvalho Franco (1999 [1969]) and Jacob Gorender (1978), to cite just a few of the outstanding scholars who have worked on this topic. Although there is not enough space here to reproduce this complex debate, we would like to revisit the argument made by Florentino (2014), who introduced a new perspective that is relevant for our purposes because it explains how such a large and cheap supply of enslaved persons could even become available.

In his study, Florentino examines the process of the 'production of the slave' in Africa. Only in exceptional cases did the coloniser or even the slave trader directly imprison and transform free persons into slaves for compulsory labour in Europe and the Americas during the nearly 400 years of the slave trade. The principal means by which slaves were produced in Africa were in fact the internal wars in Africa itself: both religious wars between Muslims and non-Muslims and wars between clans, tribes and states. As a rule, enslaved persons were taken as spoils by the victors, who used slaves as payment for goods from Europe, a good part of which consisted of war-related materials which were then used by warlords to produce more slaves. Though on a smaller scale, goods embarked in the ports of India and Southeast Asia – which were controlled by the Portuguese – were also valued and used in trading for slaves (Florentino, 2014).

Capitalism and slavery in Rio de Janeiro 35

Thus, one could say that the trilateral trade between Africa, Europe and America – and to a lesser extent also Asia – constituted a circuit of poles which was fed reciprocally, allowing for the continued expansion of capitalist accumulation. In other words, the increase in the demand for slave labour in the Americas to produce crops and metals for supplying industrial expansion in Europe also created new business opportunities for the European industrial companies which exported manufacturing goods and guns to feed those wars in Africa which 'produced' the slaves needed in the Americas.

The function of the state in this cycle of primitive accumulation is particularly relevant for our analytical interests. According to Florentino (2014: 104), without the formation of states in Africa, it would not have been possible to administer, submit and control slaves on the scale demanded by tricontinental trade:

> mass production made possible by the constant influx of slaves was linked not only to the existence of unequal relations of power between Africans themselves, but especially to the strengthening of state, the only producer of captives on a grand scale. It is thus not surprising that during the boom of the trade, the bulk of African societies without a state were left outside of the main axes of the slave trade.

We would also like to underscore Florentino's thorough analysis (2014) of the profitability of the slave trade. His study uncovers underexplored dimensions in the processes of primitive accumulation inherent to the trade. As he explains, the trade, seen from the perspective of the slave traders, carried great financial risks, as the commercialised 'commodity' was permanently subject to sickness and death. Based on the secondary literature, the author estimates that up to 50% of the enslaved persons died between their capture in the interior of Africa, transport to the port and their sojourn there while waiting for the embarkation of the vessel, and their departure for the transatlantic voyage. Moreover, in the port of origin and even more often during the voyage, there were frequent cases of the 'cargo' being stolen, particularly by pirates, most of whom were French. Deaths and illnesses during the voyage were also common. According to Florentino (2014: 154 s), the death of slaves transported to the port of Rio de Janeiro declined in the period he studied (1790–1830) from almost 9% to around 5% for slave ships on the Congolese–Angolan coast, starting in 1820, and from around 23% to about 13% in the case of slave ships on the Indian coast. The difference is explained by the respective amount of time it took ships to reach their destination, 33 to 40 days in the first case and up to 76 days in the second case.

The investments required for this business were significant, involving 'the purchase or lease of ships, equipping the ship's specialised personnel – masters, boatswains, surgeons and sailors, the latter of whom were almost always slaves – with specialised instruments and, most importantly, products such as fabrics, gunpowder, firearms, tobacco and spirits, all of which made the slave expeditions extremely costly' (Florentino, 2014: 154 s). Additionally, the enterprise involved a large network of individuals and companies such as

36   *Capitalism and slavery in Rio de Janeiro*

shipyards, suppliers of goods to be traded, insurance companies, intermediaries, etc. It also implied a long transnational chain of relations and functions, ranging from capture in the interior of Africa to the sale of slaves in the port of Rio de Janeiro. All of these risks and imponderabilities as well as the large number of economic agents to be remunerated beg the question of how the slave trade could be as lucrative as it was. Moreover, how could the final price of a slave in Rio de Janeiro be low enough that even less wealthy free men in Brazil could afford a slave?

Florentino offers a convincing explanation based on violence – or, in our terms, expropriations – as an essential factor in guaranteeing the trade would be lucrative. The object of expropriation, in this case, was the very lives of the people who were enslaved. These lives were stolen in the interior of Africa to be integrated into the circuit of mercantile, global capital accumulation. The payment for the goods exchanged for the slaves in African ports in a way remunerated the work of those who had transformed human lives into a slave commodity, but not the lives themselves which were wrenched from those who had received them by birth. These lives were now a good with enormous value, one which was transferred to the victors of war, without any cost to the latter, save for the costs related to war. Therefore, slaves passed into the hands of African slave merchants at a low cost and were acquired by international traders in African ports in exchange for goods that barely covered the cost of their enslavement itself and some profit, let alone the costs of biologically and socially producing the enslaved person. In Florentino's words (2014: 164):

> From the perspective of the trader from Rio, the formula in this circuit can be represented as M–C (money vs commodity), C–C (commodity vs commodity), C–M' (commodity vs more money than was initially invested) [...] [where] the exchange C–C was not in itself an equivalent trade (in hours–labour); force, and thus unpaid social work, constituted a primary form of 'production' of the captive.[1]

In his meticulous study of fortunes, investments and trading slaves, Florentino concludes that the slave trading business was the most dynamic sector of Rio de Janeiro's economy and possibly of all the economy of the colony, and later the Brazilian empire (in the period of 1790–1830). Not surprisingly, the major slave traders constituted the most powerful group of Rio de Janeiro's elite at the time. The dynamism of the city was to a large extent due to their investments in the real estate market, credit activities for other economic sectors and in other commercial activities such as houses of commerce and cabotage. The traders, especially the largest of them, were also influential political actors, occupying various positions of prominence in the state apparatus.

The inventories of the most powerful traders and their families show that the business affairs of the slave trade established in the market of Rio de Janeiro were not restricted to Brazil or even South America. Indeed, there were traders whose commercial and financial relations 'spanned from Rio de Janeiro itself to

Santa Catarina, Bahia and Pernambuco in Brazil to great international commercial centres such as Lisbon, Porto, London, Hamburg, Amsterdam, Goa, Luanda, Benguela and Mozambique' (Florentino, 2014: 203).

The international financial connections of slave traders did not cease to exist after the prohibition of the trade. On the contrary, payments made via redeemable titles abroad seem to have been a sure way to – illegally – purchase newly enslaved Africans:

> Considering the years 1841–1850 alone, it is clear that nearly 335 thousand Africans were illegally imported into the empire, representing a value equivalent to 28% of the total of the Brazilian legal imports in the same period. Payments for this slave contraband were carried out in the dark, in letters of exchange sent by commissaries of the landowners to be confiscated, in favour of the traders, in the major importing houses of Brazilian products in Lisbon, Porto, New York and London.
>
> (Alencastro, 1997: 36)

Slavery also represented an important motor of the domestic economy. At the turn of the 19th century, the Brazilian colony already exhibited a considerable internal market: 85% of its total production was destined for internal consumption. The main commercial route overland at the time was the connection between Rio de Janeiro and the captaincy of Minas Gerais, which even after the exhaustion of its gold mines continued to be the most robust economic region of the colony, producing primarily for the internal market.[2] The largest international slave traders in Rio de Janeiro, as in other Brazilian port cities, controlled 'the entire business chain in the internal market', supplying slaves, called 'pieces from Africa – by far the central commodity in exchanges' – to local wholesalers, 'that is, [to] local merchants capable of paying for large lots with money or commodities of high liquidity accepted by traders and [capable of] reselling the slaves at a profit in the interior' (Caldeira, 2011: 178). In the context of this internal trade fuelled by mule armies, a petite bourgeoisie prospered, as Caldeira describes (2011: 179):

> The physical link between the big traders and the local wholesalers was made by the muleteers, hucksters or brokers – those figures who directed the commercial caravans that took the products from one locality to the next, who purchased and sold in the hinterlands. To command them, it was necessary to have sufficient capital to be able to afford the cargo and its transport. They distributed slaves and [imported] goods on their journey there and brought back agricultural and artisanal goods and livestock – these were supposed to have enough value to provide profit for them as well as for the slave provider upon the return of the caravans to their point of departure.

Now we move on to analyse some of the political decisions and regulations that created the conditions for the port of Rio de Janeiro to acquire its nodal function in the global slave trade between the 17th and 19th centuries.

38 *Capitalism and slavery in Rio de Janeiro*

Point of departure: Governor Rui Vaz Pinto's order of 1618 and the disputes over the port district

From the very beginning, the physical space of the port has been integrated into diverse forms of primitive accumulation and marked by the close connection between the intensification of activity in the port and the development of the city (Hilf, 2012: 58 ss). Already at the beginning of the 17th century, there was a significant increase in the port activities, mainly connected to the outflow of timber and sugar produced in the plantations of the Guanabara Bay, but also to the entry of slaves and imported goods. This increase brought Governor Rui Vaz Pinto to decree an order which established the employment of black slaves[3] in the loading and unloading of ships (Lamarão, 2006: 22–23).

This was clearly a mechanism whose goal was to seize the space for generating and concentrating profit seeing as the loading and unloading of commodities in the space of the port remained restricted to the owners of slaves or, as we will see, to one owner in particular. At the same time, this order not only confirmed the presence of black slaves in urban labour, but also settled them in the port district which, until then, had served as a port of entry for slaves. As such, it represented just the beginning of regular stowing services and established its legal regime, that is, the privilege or rather monopoly over it, since the right to execute services was delegated to a private concessionary: the governor's brother (Lamarão, 2006: 22). Note that in this type of expropriation, the state operates as an instrument of market protection in order to benefit one person in particular.

Parallel to the regulation of port services and activities, all of the area was subject to conflicts among residents, cameral officials and royal functionaries in the course of the 17th and the first half of the 18th century, as shown by Bicalho (2007). She argues that such conflicts were mainly ignited by three interest groups in the region: the city council, the proprietors of the land in the port area and the Crown. Firstly, the emphyteusis and laudemium paid when selling land in the port district were a major source of revenue for the city council.[4] Further, the strategic location of the area for commercial transactions offered its new proprietors privileged economic conditions, since they could take advantage of the territory to control legal and illegal maritime commerce. Finally, the Crown took into account that the invasion of the area, as well as the construction of buildings by new residents, implied losses to the treasury and impaired the defence of the city, as it could block both revenue stemming from customs (for facilitating the outflow of goods by means of private clandestine negotiations) and the circulation of military personnel and transport (obstructed by certain constructions).

The first record of these disputes was a judgement issued by the city council around the middle of the 17th century, which authorised the sale of navy properties in order to gain resources for the construction of a fort. In 1646, this sale, which also permitted the new proprietors to construct homes, did not meet with any opposition whatsoever on the part of the royal officials. It was only in 1698 that opposition arose when, in the form of a letter, the governor general of Bahia (then the capital) established that he and only he could concede navy properties

Capitalism and slavery in Rio de Janeiro 39

and that any act of sale not ordered by him himself would be considered void (Bicalho, 2007: 8–9).

Some decades later, in 1725, the conflict became even more heated. The Commissioner of the Royal Estate of Rio de Janeiro reported to King John V, then king of Portugal, that the houses and other buildings constructed were advancing over the beaches to such an extent that they impeded the docking of vessels, hindered the business of the customs house and the barracks and considerably diminished the area of the royal warehouses and munitions storage. At the end of his letter, the commissioner requested a royal order to demolish the constructions between the sea and the public buildings of the Crown as well as to suspend the practice of presenting gifts to the city council. Before this dispute, the king requested a report from the governor general of Rio de Janeiro, who not only corroborated the commissioner's arguments, but emphasised the detriment that such buildings were causing to intercontinental commerce by hampering port services (Bicalho, 2007: 9–10).

Summoned by the king for a response to these allegations, the city council defended the buildings by citing the already-mentioned importance of sales as a source of their own revenue, as well as the residents' rights over the territory (Bicalho, 2007: 10). In these arguments, one notes the recourse to a notion of justice based on a principle of compensation. In accordance with these arguments, the residents, by virtue of their own effort, managed to transform an empty and marshy area into an urban space, which came to be fundamental for the development of business in the port.

The strife described above, as well as the decree ordered by Governor Rui Vaz Pinto, reveal a complex web of relations between public and private actors that constitute the process of accumulation. During the entire 17th century, the favouring of Pinto's brother in the execution of stowing services, the employment of enslaved black labourers and the alliance between the city council and the landholders in the port's surroundings all point towards synergies between the public and private sectors, which enabled accumulation in various dimensions: accumulation by exploiting slave labour in the port, the collection of pecuniary assets and the occupation and transformation of the space. There thus existed a public–private partnership in a broad sense which permitted the capitalist seizure of the entire zone.[5]

Furthermore, as can be surmised from the justifications given by the city council, such seizure made wide use of the rhetorical concept of 'vacant lands' for justifying expropriation. The violent character of this rhetoric in the process of expropriating land becomes evident in the fact that, as demonstrated by recent archaeological investigations, the port district was still occupied by indigenous groups in the 17th century (Tavares, 2012: 124–125). In this way, 'vacant land' was a linguistic device which played a fundamental role in the exercise of colonial power and violence in favour of primitive accumulation. It arbitrarily created entitlements and transferred rights to property (between the city council and the residents) that, in fact, served to expropriate the local population and plunder their vital space.

40 *Capitalism and slavery in Rio de Janeiro*

As we have seen, beginning at the end of the 17th century, more specifically, from 1698, we already see the first cracks in this public–private synergy, particularly as royal employees questioned the private buildings in the port zone. This occurred simultaneous to the Portuguese Crown's concern for regulating the marines of the city-ports of America (Bicalho, 2007, 8–10) as well as for promoting international commerce. The beginning of the 18th century was correspondingly marked by a policy geared towards consolidating the integration of the port into the mercantile economy. For this, the preceding conditions for accumulation (nepotism in stowing services and sales of property and specific buildings) were insufficient and even became barriers to the continuity of accumulation.

However, this new phase of capitalist expansion did not imply the renouncement of public–private partnerships. On the contrary, the resolution of the strife between the residents, city council representatives and King John V's functionaries indicate the need to reconcile private and public actors. Correspondingly, at the end of 1726, the king ruled in favour of the city council's arguments regarding the maintenance of the existing buildings, thus countering the interests of the commissioner. Yet on 10 December of the same year the King did yield to some of the commissioner's requests and by enacting a royal charter which proclaimed that 'from this point forth … none shall extend [his land] toward the sea, nor shall he construct houses on the beaches up to the end of Valongo' (Bicalho, 2007: 10). Therefore, the continuity of accumulation demanded not only breaking an old pattern, but also creating a new pattern of public–private relations. This was linked to the inauguration of a new stage of the mercantile expansion of capitalism based on a new panorama of regulatory interventions in the commodification processes of the port zone.

Expansion of port traffic and transfer of the capital to Rio de Janeiro: the decree of 8 June 1763

In the course of the second half of the 18th century, the discovery of considerable deposits of gold and later diamonds in Minas Gerais increased the importance of the port and the city of Rio de Janeiro. Due to the latter's closer proximity (than the port of Salvador in Bahia) and the previously existing roads (the so-called Old Path, via the Port of Paraty, and the New Path, opened in 1707), a regular flow of commodities began between Rio de Janeiro and Minas Gerais (Honorato, 2008: 31). This brought about a significant increase in the frequency of metropolitan ships in the port transporting gold to Europe and bringing foodstuffs, fabrics and slaves to Brazil (Honorato, 2008: 31). While Rio's port was becoming the main commercial junction with the metropolis, the city was expanding economically, physically and demographically, becoming in just a few decades a kind of 'political, administrative and military centre for the South Atlantic' for the colonial Portuguese Empire (Pijning, 2001: 397, see also Lamarão, 2006: 25–26; Hilf, 2012: 59).

The circulation of riches in the port zone and the city of Rio de Janeiro created new possibilities for illegal commercial activities in the region – among them, already in the first years of the 18th century, simple theft and piracy. French pirate ships constituted a frequent threat to the population of the city and to the estates

Capitalism and slavery in Rio de Janeiro 41

and sugar plantations located on the coast of Rio de Janeiro. Two incursions are particularly worth noting due to their degree of organisation. In 1710, the French pirate Jean-François Duclerc, commanding a fleet of 6 ships and 1,200 men, ransacked estates and sugar plantations and mills in the coastal zone and invaded the city by land, but was repelled and defeated by the inhabitants and military in the service of the Portuguese Crown. Duclerc was imprisoned and executed. In retaliation for his death, a successful action was commanded by the French pirate Duguay-Trouin a year later. Commanding a fleet of 18 vessels and more than 5,000 men as part of an initiative 'financed by different French shipowners and shareholders' (Figueiredo, 2005: 44), the pirate entered via the Guanabara Bay and invaded and occupied the city of Rio de Janeiro for 50 days. The pirates plundered everything they could and only left the city after receiving a monumental ransom:

> A pillage ensued. Once the raiders secured control of Rio, Duguay-Trouin opened negotiations over a ransom to free the city. Demands included stocks of gold and coinage held in local reserves as well as boxes of sugar and livestock. Ultimately, nearly all the city's wealth was depleted. To add insult to injury, the French offered the city's merchants the opportunity to buy back the ransacked merchandise.
>
> (Williams et al., 2016: 30)

Upon his return to France, Duguay-Trouin was celebrated as a national hero and was compensated for his particularly successful venture with the post of lieutenant general of the French navy (Williams et al., 2016: 30).

Besides these spectacular episodes, contraband and illegal commerce were a constitutive element of the commercial activities evolving in the port. As Pijning (2001) illustrates, the border between legal, illegal and tolerated activities was quite tenuous during the whole of the 18th century. The Portuguese Crown itself was ambivalent: while they condemned illegal trade in their colony which sidestepped due taxes, they tolerated and even stimulated illegal commerce with Spanish colonies, from which stocks of silver originated.

The prohibition of non-Portuguese vessels from anchoring in Brazilian ports, in effect until 1808, was also applied in an inconsistent manner. According to Pijning (2001), the Portuguese authorities were particularly tolerant of English and Dutch ships, given the protection that these two countries provided Portugal, especially in its disputes with Spain and France. Hence, in practice, the existing prohibitions did not create unrelenting impediments for commercial activities; instead, they created new business opportunities for port functionaries and colonial authorities at various levels, who used their discretionary power to extract personal advantages from the negotiations conducted with the foreign merchants. The same occurred with the local commercial activities which took place at the port:

> The governor, servicemen, customs officials and the municipal councillors had jurisdiction over different areas, designated according to the given form of commerce. The most disputed area was the pier, which all four groups

42   *Capitalism and slavery in Rio de Janeiro*

sought to control. Here, pedlars, merchants, fishermen, soldiers, sailors from coastal ships and officials tried to gain their share of the illegal trade. The control exercised by one administrator over this zone could easily be transformed into extra revenue. For example, the fishermen who arrived with their catch at the beaches of Rio de Janeiro were forced to pay one tenth to those who commissioned them, a levy which was collected by the local guard.

(Pijning, 2001: 404)

The decision to make Rio de Janeiro the new capital was established by the decree issued by the Marquis of Pombal on 8 June 1763. In addition to amending the decree issued by King Joseph I on 11 May of the same year, which named the Count of Cunha the new viceroy of Brazil, Pombal's decree also determined that the Count's residence was to be the city of Rio de Janeiro (Da Silva, 2012: 55). This entanglement between port and city stimulated important changes in the port zone, including the opening of new routes, buildings related to new piers, arsenals etc. These, in turn, favoured the urban development of the city (Cardoso et al., 1987: 27).

To summarise, from the end of the 17th century to the end of the 18th century, the port of Rio de Janeiro, in its first established location near the Hill of Castelo, was the scene of entangled accumulation in all of the three functions described above, namely: in its function-end (which facilitated the integration of Minas Gerais into the mercantile economy), in the area of the port itself (with the optimisation of port services) and in the relation between the port and the city (with the occupation of the surroundings of the port). In the realm of mercantile accumulation, one sees an articulation between these three dimensions insofar as Brazilian integration into the global dynamic of accumulation increased profits in the exploitation of port services and stimulated successive occupations in the perimeter of the port – both in the seizure of external areas not yet urbanised and the expropriation of an 'exterior' that did not keep up with the changes in the port flows and was thus devaluated. This is accompanied by a change in the relations of property in various parishes, where farms were converted into villas, shifting the slave labour previously employed in agriculture to urban labour (Honorato, 2008: 36 ss, 59; Lamarão, 2006: 38).

The orders of the second Marquis of Lavradio (1769–1779): commerce and disciplining slaves in the port of Rio de Janeiro

From the moment that Rio de Janeiro became Brazil's principal commercial junction, the port–city relation has been seen as being both convergent and fruitful, combining an increased movement of ships, intensified commercial flows, technological development and expanded urbanisation (Santos, 1995: 257–268). In the port zone, this symbiotic trajectory has meant the accumulation of capital by seizing space, which has taken the form of the construction of buildings (from residential to offices and storage), the opening of roads, increasing population

Capitalism and slavery in Rio de Janeiro 43

density and the acceleration of local commerce (Honorato, 2008: 130). Within these transformations generated by the port–city confluence of Rio de Janeiro, the most important by far was the order decreed by the Second Marquis of Lavradio (Viceroy of Brazil between 1769 and 1779) on 12 April 1774, which made reference to the 1758 Statute of the City Council, the legislation which governed the move of the slave market from Direita Street to Valongo Wharf (Honorato, 2008: 34, 73–74; Lamarão, 2006: 27). With this, all of the slave traders from the most powerful to the so-called 'middlemen' were transferred to the perimeter of the port (Honorato, 2008: 64 ss).[6]

In contrast to the previously described act privileging nepotism ordered by Governor Rui Vaz Pinto in 1618, the new order stimulated autonomous economic actors. To enable the circulation of goods and capital, various urban projects were initiated. Mello (2003: 31) cites for instance land reclamations, the extension of dry areas, the inauguration of streets in order to facilitate movement around the slave market and the creation of Livramento Street, which permitted the occupation of the new district (Lamarão, 2006: 27; Mello, 2003: 30–31). The local population regularly frequented the slave market, turning the area into one of the most bustling spots in Rio de Janeiro (Haag, 2011: 26; Pereira, 2007: 76).

The increase in the capital's transit is seen in the elevated number of establishments trading slaves, then known as 'meat houses', which the area came to house – close to 50 in all (Pereira, 2007: 76; Hilf, 2012: 61). Based on visitors' reports, Honorato (2008: 83) calculates that in 1826, each one of the 'houses' contained close to 2000 slaves for sale. Moreover, as Pereira (2007: 76) shows, the entire zone was occupied by centres dedicated to commerce, importing, exporting and storage. Ship movement in the area was constant (Pereira, 2007: 76). As the literature confirms, all of this commercial excitement spurred urban expansion to the north of the city, where the accumulation of capital generated by intense economic activity could occur outside of the limits in which it arose (Pereira, 2007: 76).

The economic momentum generated by the relocation of the market was evidently associated with the purchase and sale of enslaves. Parallel to this activity, one sees the simultaneous development of techniques used to repress and discipline the enslaved and expropriated black population. The justification given for these techniques was primarily sanitary vigilance and public health (Haag, 2011: 25; Hilf, 2012: 60; Honorato, 2008: 68 ss). The debate underpinning the 1758 Statute of the City Council, which stipulated the move of the slave market to Valongo, was corroborated by medical experts. They claimed that the illnesses present in the city were brought by 'new blacks' – as the recently arrived Africans were called – and diffused among the residents due to their transport and exposition for sale in the city centre (Honorato, 2008: 68).

Correspondingly, the Marquis of Lavradio's order, which ratified the statute, proposed to combat

> the terrible custom that every [black] who arrived at the ports from the Coast of Africa, immediately after disembarking, came into the city, through the public streets and main thoroughfares, not only full of infinite maladies, but

44 *Capitalism and slavery in Rio de Janeiro*

naked, and with the quality of folks who have no learning, the same that any other brute savage in the middle of the street sitting on some planks there laid out doing whatever nature impelled, causing not only the greatest stench in the said streets and its surroundings, but being also the most horrible spectacle eyes could see.

(Marquês do Lavradio 1779,
quoted according to Williams et al., 2016: 42)[7]

To implement this order, as soon as the market was brought to Valongo, the city council was made responsible for the health inspection of the new arrivals and, when they were diagnosed with illnesses, determined that they would be quarantined in the city's warehouses and lazarettes (Honorato, 2008: 115). Due to the profit made by the traders, the scarcity of doctors and the popular belief of the healing power of phlebotomists, 'treatment' consisted in bloodletting carried out by barbers, generally resulting in death (Haag, 2011: 25; Honorato, 2008: 116).

Following the move of the slave market, the Marquis of Lavradio decreed another order governing the transferral of the Cemetery of Pretos Novos to Valongo. Along with this order, the rule was established that

[s]laves who were not sold were not to leave Valongo, not even after their decease.

(Pereira, 2007: 74; see also Haag, 2011: 26)

The cemetery functioned from 1772 to 1830 and served the purpose of interring the remains of African men, women and children who had died following their entry into the Guanabara Bay and thus before they were sold on the market (Carvalho, 2007: 8). Using the Register of Deaths in the Parish of Santa Rita from 1824 to 1830, Pereira (2007: 100) was able to confirm a total of 6,119 interred slaves. Yet this source does not reveal the number of slaves buried in the period from 1772 to 1824, the period which saw the intensified arrival of ships transporting slaves in the port and thus an increase in the number of persons who arrived at the port dead, or who perished just after arriving. Based on more recent archaeological excavations, it is estimated that the cemetery received more than 20,000 corpses (Haag, 2011: 26). This high mortality rate reveals the conditions that those women, men and children were subjected to on the ships, in the lazarettes and on the market.

The aforementioned excavations reveal a disproportionately high number of skeletons belonging to children and teenagers, indicating that this group was particularly susceptible to death during the voyage and while waiting for sale in the port (Williams et al., 2016: 42). In the registers of slave arrivals in the port between 1795 and 1830, there was a ratio of 3.2 men to every woman and about 4% of the arrivals were children under the age of ten. The number of adolescents between 10 and 14 years of age was particularly significant given that 'for each group of ten captives being transported, nine were between ten and thirty-four years old' (Florentino, 2014: 60).

Capitalism and slavery in Rio de Janeiro 45

According to the logic of primitive accumulation, this process relates to the attainment of profit by the sale of commodities (slaves) with the formation of unequal social relations through expropriations and the disciplining of the labour power (Dörre, 2015: 25). The Valongo Complex was thus a fundamental place in the long line of subordination of slave labour. At the port, a punitive model of sanitary intervention prevailed. At the market, however, this model resorted to the penal tradition of social control by employing tactics such as abuse, physical and moral torture, punishments, withholding food and care, murder, etc.

The royal family in Rio de Janeiro

Fleeing from the expansionist wars of Napoleon Bonaparte in Europe, the seat of the Portuguese Crown and the royal family were transferred to Rio de Janeiro, arriving in Brazil in 1808, where they remained for 13 years. It is quite likely that in no other phase of its history had the city been marked by transformations as radical as the ones that took place in this period. The globalising impulse which the city was given in the period was monumental: following the arrival of Prince John, later King John VI, who governed the colonial Portuguese Empire as proxy for his mother (then known as *Maria the Insane* on account of her mental illness), Rio de Janeiro experienced a unique and paradoxical situation. Instead of just being the capital of a colony, it became, at least temporarily, the capital of a kingdom, which extended from South America to Europe and from Europe to Asia and Africa, as Silva (2011: 25f) adroitly describes:

> In 1808, Rio de Janeiro was transformed into the Portuguese capital overnight. At the head of the Empire. The metropolitan state institutions now had to be recreated on the American side, from the Atlantic. Or rather, it was necessary to reassemble the state, which had arrived by ship, incomplete and in pieces. The old regime, which was only slowly opening up to anti-aristocratic and liberal thought, was transplanted in Brazil. Even the representations of the theatre of power were reproduced in Rio de Janeiro with the contribution of French artists, [...] In short, it was sought to repeat Lisbon, even if just in a scenery made of wood, cloth and paper.

The presence of the royal family and the court, together with an enormous apparatus, composed of thousands of civil servants, artists, intellectuals and craftsmen, represented not only a repositioning of Rio de Janeiro on the global map of power relations, but also a profound reorganisation of the local relations of power. In this context, the local rulers quite literally had to make room for the Portuguese powerholders. In addition to posts and public mandates, the local rulers, in accordance with the decree of the Portuguese Crown which remained in effect until 1818, were forced to yield their residences whenever a member of the Crown wished to reside there.

The attempt to reconstruct a distant Lisbon to the greatest extent possible in Rio de Janeiro caused a turnaround in the city's limited infrastructure and its urban

46 *Capitalism and slavery in Rio de Janeiro*

colonial cityscape. New squares were constructed, old ones were extended, new public buildings were erected and in the span of just few years, a royal library, a museum, an academy of arts, a botanical garden, an opera and a government palace were created, among other institutions which aimed to disseminate 'European culture' (Schwarcz, 2012: 256 ff).

The presence of the court with its conventions and rituals, along with the opening of Brazilian ports to foreign ships, also brought a profound transformation in local forms of sociability. Women belonging to the local elite, who had until then only gone into the streets with their heads and faces covered or in litters carried by slaves, began to imitate Portuguese nobility and even Carlota Joaquina, the king's wife, known for customs at that time considered eccentric and libertarian, such as riding her horse in public spaces. 'An important proportion of the process of modernisation, Europeanisation and Gallicisation of Rio de Janeiro which would gradually infect other Brazilian towns' was hence attributed to women (Silva, 2011: 52).

The new liberty won by women of the elite contrasted with the situation of enslaved black women. Though many of them were allowed to work as pedlars, for example, they were still the property of men and women who disposed of their time, labour and bodies. This contrast was one of the many paradoxes that marked everyday life in Rio during the years in which it acted as the capital of a global empire. Even after independence, declared by the very son of the Portuguese king, Peter I, the first Brazilian Emperor, local society continued to be profoundly segmented, stratified and limited.

Accordingly, as Silva (2011: 57 ss) shows, the royal and local nobility (the latter still in a process of formation) as well as the commercial elite, with its slave traders and the large landowners, were at the top of the social pyramid. These groups were in constant dispute over wealth, power and influence. Below them were the high-ranking functionaries of the state, military officers and liberal professions. Then came the white middle class, made up of mid-ranking functionaries and military officers, pharmacists, and shopkeepers and one rung below them were craftsmen and diverse service providers. At the bottom of the social pyramid were very poor whites, free blacks and slaves. The slaves were differentiated according to whether they were African or Brazilian-born as well as according to their occupation – for instance, whether they were *escravos de ganho*, who worked for third parties paying their masters a fixed daily amount, or domestic slaves who lived in a wide range of conditions depending on their owner's wealth. Mestizos were represented in all social classes and, especially in the case of those with fairer skin, could have even studied in Coimbra or Montpellier and circulated among the local elite.

The complexity of social stratification in Rio de Janeiro and the overlap and interpenetration of labour regimes are evident above all in the generalised practice among the small owners to rent their slaves for a wide range of services. Drawing from advertisements from contemporary newspapers, Alencastro (1997: 64s) shows that it was particularly common to rent female domestic slaves in the post-natal period to breastfeed children of the elite. These instances illustrate that

Capitalism and slavery in Rio de Janeiro 47

slaves were not excluded from the process of capital accumulation and testify to the insufficiency of dualist interpretations which identify slave labour as irrelevant for capitalism.

In the Rio de Janeiro of the first decades of the 19th century, slaves only found a possible space of liberty at celebrations as well as religious city or street festivals:

> Liberty with the taste of Africa, given that it was on the street that they found those from the nation from which they themselves had been kidnapped. Often enough, there were a few recently arrived countrymen with fresh news from their homeland.
>
> (Silva, 2011: 60)

The maintenance of this diverse and hierarchical society implied a combination of daily concessions and negotiations over social positions. These negotiations included violence and repression both by the state and by private actors such as foremen and slave owners. The rigid methods of discipline included prison and severe corporal punishment of slaves who tried to run away as well as repression for those who had practised their own cultural and religious activities. Yet large rebellions, such as the Malê Revolt of 1835 in Salvador, in Bahia, did not take place in Rio de Janeiro during the 19th century. Having said that, attempts to run away were not uncommon as shown by recurring runaway slave ads in local newspapers from the period. In fact, very close to the city, relatively long-lasting settlements called *quilombos* were established by slaves who had succeeded in escaping. Quilombos and their inhabitants, as a general rule, maintained regular contact with slaves and freedmen in the city, who for their part helped them by offering temporary refuge, buying their goods and sending them necessary supplies (Williams et al., 2016: 75).

The entry of slaves into the port of Rio de Janeiro grew at a dizzying rate after the arrival of the royal family and continued growing even after the return of the royal family to Portugal in 1821. Even the new independent state had its own slaves. Accordingly, the arrival of ships transporting enslaved Africans to Rio de Janeiro continued to increase in the period and even after independence was declared in 1822: between 1826 and 1930, an average of 96 ships arrived per year, or about 2 ships a week, each carrying approximately 400 slaves (Florentino, 2014: 45). Interventions in the port zone, whether in the form of regulations or public works, were equally numerous.

Prescriptions regarding the health of newly arrived Africans: the sanitary policy of the Crown in the port district and the (private) Lazarette of Valongo

As seen, the initial years subsequent to the Marquis of Lavradio's decree followed a model of sanitation executed directly by the municipality (without delegation) that sought to confine the sufferers of illnesses, excluding them from any form of social contact. Later, this model became a much more complex structure. The

48 *Capitalism and slavery in Rio de Janeiro*

Statute of 22 January 1810 mandated that embarkations carrying slaves anchor twice: in Cove of Boa Viagem or in Paço, where they were inspected by health officials who determined the period of quarantine, and on the Island of Bom Jesus, where both healthy and ill passengers were confined and selected for different destinations. Those who perished – and the mortality rate was very high – left the island directly for the Cemetery of Pretos Novos (Tavares, 2012: 83).

Slave traders sent representatives to the prince regent, claiming that the two obligatory anchorages led to financial losses due to the unnecessary delay, the risk of infecting healthy passengers and, supposedly, the lacking gravity of the sicknesses, which, according to the traders, could be treated directly on the ships or in the houses of commerce. Though each of these claims were contested by the chief medical officer (Provedor Mor da Saúde) based on sanitary issues, a consensus was reached which led to the creation of the Lazarette of Valongo on the Hill of Nossa Senhora da Saúde, according to a royal proclamation from 23 September 1810.[8] With this, a complex of services linked to human trafficking was formed in the area of Valongo, comprising

> the pier, where recently arrived Africans disembarked; the market on Valongo Street, where those in good condition were sold …; the lazarette in Gamboa, where those who were infected or already dying were quarantined and the Cemetery of Pretos Novos on Pedro Ernesto Street, where the dead were interred.
>
> (Lima et al., 2016: 307)

However, there were no substantial changes in the precarious treatment offered to the slaves, even by the standards of the time, and mortality rates among the sick remained extraordinarily high (Pereira, 2007: 106). The novelty consisted in adjusting the punitive model of sanitary intervention to the standards of accumulation in the port area, consolidated by the order to transfer the slave market. It was a stimulus for autonomous economic actors. The friendly denouement of the feud between the chief medical officer and the slave traders mandated that, following the proclamation cited above, the Lazarette of Valongo be constructed by three of the principal traders in Brazil registered in the Royal Council of Commerce and that the territory be awarded according to the price agreed upon by audit.[9] The same proclamation declared them proprietors of the Lazarette. For their services, the remaining traders were to pay 400 *réis* per confined slave. This sum, said the chief medical officer, was a compensation for the expenses in purchasing land and constructing the lazarette (Honorato, 2008: 105 ss; Pereira, 2007: 106 ss).

In consonance with the above-mentioned porous border between state and private actors, public–private partnerships in a broader sense were fundamental for the entangled accumulation analysed also here. Accordingly, the royal proclamation of 1810 delegated the provision of health services exclusively to three slave traders and ordered that private actors guarantee a compensation, that is, the other traders were obligated to send sick, newly arrived enslaved Africans to the lazarette. As Pereira (2007: 108) demonstrates, this theoretical framework was adjusted to the slaveholder logic in 18th-century Rio, which was to promote the diversification of economic enterprises. This diversification was part of the process of expansion of mercantile capitalism that, in the port district, materialised in the occupation of the territory of the Hill of Nossa Senhora da Saúde by the entrepreneurs of the slave market.

Delegating health services to three traders also exempted the state from the high costs, both economic (the treatment of the many disembarked slaves who were ill) and political (the constant complaints made against the chief medical officer), generated by the implementation of the sanitary policies.[10] This policy, also carried out by private actors, reinforced its character of disciplining the labour slave.

The new lazarette had an elevated number of deaths and did not update the treatments already provided at the Island of Bom Jesus. To avoid financial losses on the part of the slave traders and given the widespread belief in the healing powers of bloodletting, there was a complete absence of doctors in Valongo under the aegis of the private legal regime. Thus, sick Africans were handed over to the care of barbers and veterinarians (Honorato, 2008: 116; 2006: 3). According to Tavares (2012: 81), the point of the quarantine was not to cure the slaves, but rather to wait and let destiny decide the path the life of the enslaved individual would take.

The lazarette did however introduce a new component into the process of disciplining the slave population. On 28 July 1810, a statute was announced which attended to the claim that the healthy, newly arrived enslaved Africans did not need to pass through the quarantine and could be taken directly to the market warehouses (Honorato, 2008: 105). As a result, a division between the sick and the healthy was established and with it their confinement differentiated, either in the lazarette or in the warehouses. On the one hand, both brought the valorisation of commercial capital, via the payment of the recollection fee to the owners of the lazarette or sale; on the other, they intensified the suffering caused by separation and the impossibility of caring for a loved one as their health declined (Pereira, 2013: 233). Correspondingly, the new public–private partnerships in a broader sense reflected a punitive model of sanitary intervention shared by the power of the state and that of the market. This model was necessary both for subjection to slave labour and the expansion of established entangled accumulation.

Accumulation and discipline between public and private legal regimes: from bloody penal legislation to the inefficacy of the Charter of 24 November 1813

This repressive structure was broadened at the slave market where, as mentioned, the methods of the traditional penal model of social control were widely applied. To give an idea of how this model functioned in Valongo, it suffices to revisit the various travellers' reports extensively documented in the research done by Pereira (2007; 2013), Tavares (2012) and Honorato (2008; 2006).

According to these reports, men, women and children were put up for sale just as any other consumer good, along with foodstuffs and other commodities

50   *Capitalism and slavery in Rio de Janeiro*

(Pereira, 2013: 225, 240). Many of the travellers emphasised that the heads of the slaves were shaved and that all were practically nude, with only a piece of cloth covering their waist (Honorato, 2008: 77–78; Tavares, 2012: 93; Pereira, 2007: 240). One report written by the Spaniard Juan Francisco Aguirre in 1783 noted that the Africans were constantly beaten (Pereira, 2013: 225; 2007: 76).

In his report and others from Charles Brand, Henry Chamberlain, G. W. Freireyss and Johann Moritz Rugendas, one reads that the practices of 'confinement' subjected slaves to enclosure and seclusion, the same methods used on livestock (Honorato, 2008: 77–78, 85; Tavares, 2012: 19, 54). The houses belonging to the market, for their part, were described by Rugendas as being 'true stables' in which, according to Brand, the slaves lived and slept on the floors 'like livestock in every imaginable way' (Honorato, 2008: 77–78, 82). One of these aspects, Freireyss noted, was a mark of branding (Honorato, 2008: 79; Tavares, 2012: 104), while Chamberlain told of how, at the moment of sale, the captives were obligated to 'show their teeth, violently stretch their arms and legs, run, and scream to demonstrate their good health' (Honorato, 2008: 85). Alongside the market, in order to facilitate commercial activities, the state created depositories in the Warehouse of Valongo, where slaves could be collected after their display for sale (Honorato, 2008: 34).

Further, there was no restriction whatsoever on selling members of a family separately, so that children were torn from their families and couples were often condemned to never see one another again. This practice shocked the young Charles Darwin (1959 [1913]) while passing through Rio de Janeiro in 1832, a time when the slave trade was prohibited yet still continued to occur. Internal trade – from one region of the country to another – was intensifying, so the scene Darwin detailed could be referring to this trade. While admitting that on farms such as the one he was visiting, 'I have no doubt the slaves pass happy and contented lives' (Darwin, 1959 [1913]: 20), he could not conceal his discomfort upon witnessing the sale of slaves in Rio de Janeiro (from the report, it is not possible to know where exactly he observed the scene):

> While staying at this stage, I was very nearly being an eyewitness to one of those atrocious acts which can only take place in a slave country. Owing to a quarrel and a lawsuit, the owner was on the point of taking all the women and children from the male slaves and selling them separately at the public auction in Rio. Interest, and not any feeling of compassion, prevented this act. Indeed, I do not believe the inhumanity of separating thirty families who had lived together for many years even occurred to the owner.
>
> (Darwin, 1959 [1913]: 22)

As Pereira (2013: 228) and Tavares (2012: 92) demonstrate, slaves died not only on ships and in the lazarettes, but also in the market shops during their continued exposition. The traditional penal model of social control thus extended from the public slave depositories to the market houses. In these houses, the merchants were responsible for the slaves' entire routine (Tavares, 2012: 86). This means

Capitalism and slavery in Rio de Janeiro 51

that, along with repressive state policies, a private yet authorised penal law allowed merchants to impose their own codes of behaviour and punishment. In this way, even where the traditional penal model was adopted, it was possible to find a high degree of public–private synergies. Among the 'miserable rooms' of the market and state warehouses along the pier, slaves were submitted to a permanent state of discipline and punishment.

Obviously, the punitive practices that took place in Valongo were first and foremost oriented towards a commercial vision: the transformation of the Africans into commodities capable of attracting buyers. As mentioned above, this served to discipline the slave labour following the logic of primitive accumulation. Despite some legal–political discourses demanding improvement in the living conditions of slaves to increase the merchants' revenue (Rediker, 2007: 196 ss), the state of the captive Africans never improved, nor did the number of deaths diminish.

Still, many lamented the economic losses stemming from maltreatment. Merchants complained about the enormous damage done to their businesses by the methods employed on the Island of Bom Jesus (Honorato, 2008: 102), whereas the chief medical officer defended the quarantine while guaranteeing good business for shipowners, merchants and buyers (Honorato, 2008: 104 ss). The most eloquent of these measures was the Charter of 24 November 1813 regulating the operation of cargo, transport and unloading of black women and men. It portrayed the slave as a living commercial good that needed to remain healthy to generate profit, and prescribed a series of 'improvements', including the substitution of branding with shackles, the embarkation of a surgeon so that the number of deaths would not surpass 2 or 3% of the cargo and the necessity of food, potable water, daily movement, ventilation, etc.

Despite the charter, numerous forms of evidence point to the fact that abuse, confinement and the elevated number of deaths never ceased. Firstly, the majority of the reports written by travellers described above date back to the period *following* the charter's pronouncement. Indeed, the one written by Freireyss is from 1814. Moreover, in 1815, the General Intendant of the Police sent a letter to the Court of Criminal Justice of Sé requesting a clean-up of one of the swamps of Valongo, which had turned into a corpse deposit site; it was used by merchants to avoid the costs of burying their slaves in the Cemetery of Pretos Novos. Its existence could only be justified by a high mortality rate (Pereira, 2007: 113). Additionally, studies on bones extracted from the cemetery show that they exhibited 'signs of abuse, such as fractures, infections, anaemia and deterioration' (Pereira, 2007. 134). The prevalence of anaemia in particular indicates that the slaves were held in a permanent state of malnutrition, favouring the contraction of diseases (Haag, 2011: 29).

The inefficacy of the charter can be understood in the light of the question of profitability and circulation and accumulation of capital in the commercial form of accumulation. In comparing the annual rate at which slaves entered the port with the rate of burial in the Cemetery of Pretos Novos, Pereira (2007: 113) notes that more deaths meant the necessity of importing more and more slaves. Similarly, Honorato (2008: 77; 2006: 2) ascertains that the presence of negative reports in relation to the region increased during the periods of large slave imports, all of

52 *Capitalism and slavery in Rio de Janeiro*

which, according to the author, confirms that slaves were more abused in these periods, given that excesses were more visible.

Interestingly, the traditional penal model of social control stimulated the emergence of economic enterprises that produced the means required for its execution. For instance, the establishment of manufacturers of iron objects, destined for use in the imprisonment and torture of slaves in the port district, has fundamental symbolic relevance for the development of the respective form of accumulation (Hilf, 2012: 60). This is even more so if we take into account that the establishment of these enterprises is considered a relevant factor in the occupation, urbanisation and economic movement of the region (Mello, 2003: 30–31). Employed by private penal law, the instruments of discipline not only undermined the reach of the Charter of 24 November 1813, but could also explain why it was revoked by the Charter of 26 January 1818, which substituted the demand for surgeons with black phlebotomists and reintroduced branding (Tavares, 2012: 68).

The punitive measures used against slaves were obviously not limited to recent arrivals nor to the port district itself and they did not come to an end after the official prohibition of the trade in 1831. At the same time as the punishment of slaves was a prerogative of slaves' masters, public institutions specialised in the punishment of slaves who tried to escape or committed other crimes. Two letters written by the Chief of Police of Rio de Janeiro, Eusébio de Queiroz (later the Minister of Justice of the Empire between 1848 and 1852), recollected by Williams et al. (2016: 99 ss), give an idea of how widely punitive actions were applied. The first, sent on 1 June 1833 to the city council, requested specific legislation prohibiting 'the use of the tambour in the slave dance called candomblé, which can be heard a league's distance away and attracts slaves from neighbouring farms; such meetings might give rise to the evils to which Your Lord is no stranger' (Eusébio Queiroz apud Williams et al., 2016: 100). The second, dated 30 May 1837, was directed to the administrator of the *Calabouço* (Dungeon) and demanded that all slaves incarcerated there be transferred to the new House of Corrections. It was supposedly informed by the reformist spirit as well as the wish to overcome the colonial penal system. Yet imprisoned slaves in the House of Detention

> were bound by a *libambo*, a set of iron restraints commonly used to join together a line of slaves by their hands and necks. The routine duties of the guards at the House of Correction included whippings, and the lash was a potent symbol of the inhumanity and humiliation that was transferred with enslaved people to the city's modern penal institutional.
>
> (Williams et al., 2016: 101)

The Cemetery of Pretos Novos and the devaluation of the port district

Of all the methods of discipline employed, the construction of the Cemetery of Pretos Novos is, without a doubt, the most expressive and is directly related to the strategies of accumulation in the port district and the city. Firstly, although its

Capitalism and slavery in Rio de Janeiro   53

exact size is still unknown, it was strategically located in the middle of the route between the Lazarette of Valongo and the market (Tavares, 2012: 83). Here, as detailed in the investigation carried out by Pereira (2007: 74), the corpses were interred nude without any kind of religious sacrament in mass graves and shallow ditches, so that the deceased were practically exposed to sunlight. As these bodies were visible to anyone, principally from the market, the absence of any funeral ritual or mourning was another component which diminished the dignity of recently arrived Africans (Pereira, 2007: 74).

Furthermore, according to reports from the time, the small amount of soil thrown over the innumerable corpses increased the frequency of the discovery of human remains, evidently intensifying the suffering and the fears of the living (Honorato, 2006: 4). This state of affairs was administered by the Church, which charged the merchants for burials. Along with the merchants and the state, the Church was a third (private) actor that comprised the complex of capital accumulation that was taking shape in Valongo.

Moreover, travellers' reports from the period as well as various current investigations show that, on account of the conditions described above, the cemetery was characterised by terrible odours and insalubrity (Honorato, 2006: 14; 2008: 131; Pereira, 2007: 78, 84; Tavares, 2012: 149). In 1996, archaeological studies found signs of detritus and urban refuse apparently linked to the bones in the area. Thus, new excavations, whose results were published in 2012, have assumed that the cemetery was likely transformed into a depository for rubbish in the aftermath of its closure. Nevertheless, tests based on the stratigraphic level of the human remains and the detritus confirmed that the area were used to deposit trash not only after its closure, but even during the cemetery's functioning (Tavares, 2012: 136). It is worth stressing that the stench and the insalubrity were not limited to the cemetery. According to Honorato (2006: 2), Pereira (2013: 224–224 and 240) and Tavares (2012: 93), the market was equally characterised by 'terrible odours', 'strong smells', 'a thousand filths' and 'insalubrious houses', where the slaves were compelled to 'do their business in public'. Obviously, this scenery contributed to converting the port district into a *petri dish* for the transmission of illnesses (Haag, 2001: 26; Honorato, 2006: 116).

This picture produced a fundamentally contradictory effect within the process of accumulation of the port district itself as well as its relationship with the urban and economic expansion of Rio de Janeiro. On the one hand, previously collected data show that the intensification of the movement from the port and the occupation of its surroundings impelled the development of the area and the city as a whole. On the other hand, the cruel, precarious and unsanitary conditions inherent to slavery contradictorily brought a devaluation and degradation of the area, along with its separation from the rest of the city.

This phenomenon could already be observed in the justification given for the Marquis of Lavradio's decision to transfer the slave market to Valongo (Pereira, 2007: 73–74; 2013: 223–224). His intention was clearly to 'drive the uncomfortable place of sale' outside the city centre. Based on the debate that had already involved the city chamber and the doctors of the city, the Marquis claimed that the

54   *Capitalism and slavery in Rio de Janeiro*

presence of new slaves among the new dwellings contributed to the filth, insalubrity and especially the spread of epidemics and illnesses that the slaves brought from Africa. What is more, he promised that from then on Valongo would be a more organised place and have exemplary hygiene; the spread of scourges around the city would be impeded and the death rate of slaves would diminish. Therefore, the decision was grounded in sanitary arguments. However, the conditions, structures and practices in the port district reveal that the effect of the decision was merely to shift the slave trade to the port. As the various forms of violence and insalubrity associated with this institution remained intact, the sanitary argument that justified transferring the slave market to Valongo was exclusively geared towards the valuation of the centre of the city.

In this sense, the transferral of the slave market was clearly orientated towards removing and invisibilising this commerce (which in turn devalued the space where it took place). It was driven by a hygienist policy of cleansing the zones occupied by the more privileged population of the city. In line with Tavares (2012: 54), the most obvious conclusion is that the construction of the complex in Valongo served to 'isolate the market from respectable colonial society' and 'distance it from the sight of the noblemen'. This construction imported a disjuncture and division among the districts inhabited by the subaltern popular classes and those occupied by the dominant classes.

In the case of the district of Valongo, one piece of information that is important for comprehending this process is the number of complaints and protests from the local residents, which pressured the public authorities to close the Cemetery of Pretos Novos (Pereira, 2007: 77 ss). Starting in 1820, a number of complaints to the prince regent were processed by the Court of Criminal Justice, and there were also statements by the chief medical officer. Of course, each of these acts would demand an analysis of its own. For our purposes, however, it is relevant that the cemetery resisted each and every one of the complaints and maintained a process of gradual devaluation of the dwellings in the area; these dwellings increasingly came to be occupied by poor tenants, while the rest of the districts of Rio de Janeiro (such as Lapa, Catete, Glória, Flamengo and Botafogo) served the elites, always in search of 'fresh air' (Pereira, 2007: 34).

The arrival of the royal family rendered this division all the more visible. Beginning in 1808, the number of slave imports to the port increased significantly, as did the number of the deceased buried in the cemetery and the negative travel reports concerning maltreatment and insalubrities in the market (Honorato, 2008: 74). At the same time, the royal family initiated urban policies such as the Statute of 11 June 1808, which incentivised the expansion of the city by means of diverse improvements in infrastructure (Honorato, 2008: 59). This differentiated treatment of the port district consolidated it as a space inhabited by 'poor whites, slaves selling goods and free blacks who earned their livelihood with sporadic jobs in the port' (Pereira, 2007: 34).

The cemetery and the market even resisted the Act of 7 November 1831, which freed Africans disembarked in Brazil. The trade continued illegally and was only definitively abolished following the Aberdeen Act of 1845 with which England imposed the abolition of the slave trade on Brazil. It was implemented by means of the Eusébio de Queiroz Law, promulgated in 1850 (Pereira, 2007: 129).[11]

The arrival of the Empress Tereza Cristina in Brazil in 1843 was used as an opportunity to renovate the Valongo Wharf and its surroundings, stigmatised by the commerce with slaves. The area that then came to be called The Imperatriz Wharf continued serving as a square and pier until the beginning of the 20th century, when it was banked for the construction of the new port of Rio de Janeiro. The archaeologists and researchers at the forefront of the excavations – the same ones who, beginning in 2011, revealed an important part of the structures belonging both to the Valongo Wharf (with the features conferred to it by the works of 1811) and the Imperatriz Wharf, culminating in the recognition of the area as a World Heritage Site – believe that the remodelling project of 1843 was not completed. Furthermore, the group thinks that, based on the many petitions for new interventions in the area at the end of the 19th century, the renovation of 1843 was not enough to reverse the process of 'continual degradation' of the area (Lima et al., 2016: 313).

As far as this book is concerned, it is clear that from this moment on, the area began to lose importance as a space of accumulation until the beginning of the 20th century, when it became the object of urban reforms launched by President Rodrigues Alves and mayor Pereira Passos.

Notes

1 The transaction M–C refers to the expenses associated with the preparation of the voyage and the acquisition of goods to be traded for slaves, the transaction C–C refers to the trade of commodities for slaves in the African port and the transaction C–M' refers to the sale of slaves in the port of Rio de Janeiro for a value above that which was initially invested in the preparation of the voyage.
2 *Captaincies* were the system of administrative division adopted by Portugal to rule the colony of Brazil. A *captaincy* was a form of distribution of a hereditary fief.
3 The expression was used to distinguish them from indigenous slaves, who also existed in this period. The transformation of the indigenous into Portuguese slaves was possible due to both the stimulus and instrumentalisation of internal wars between the different tribes, as shown by the case of enslavement of Africans, and to the enslavement that supposedly took place on the territory under the jurisdiction of the Jesuits, as well as the hunting and capturing expeditions into the interior. Colonial legislation remained ambivalent concerning these practices and, while recommending the liberty of indigenous peoples, accepted enslavement in cases when 'they were subjugated in a *just war*' (Gileno, 2007: 124).
4 *Emphyteusis* and *laudemium* are legal instruments, which prescribe the payment of a sum for the right to enjoy the fruits and the tenure of the property of another.
5 We are quite aware of the fact that the generalisation of the role of public–private partnerships to include non-financial regimes of capitalism runs the risk of anachronism, thus hindering any comparison of prior legal relations with contemporary categories of economic and administrative law. Nevertheless, if we consider that public–private partnerships point to entanglement between public and private actors oriented towards the creation of an adequate space for the accumulation of capital, then in this *broader* sense it could very well be possible to employ this notion to understand other historical phases of development of capitalism, as is done in the present study.

56 *Capitalism and slavery in Rio de Janeiro*

6 'Middlemen' were small merchants who bought recently arrived slaves and resold them to sugar plantation and mill owners, taking advantage of the long time it would otherwise take these owners to arrive in Rio de Janeiro (Honorato, 2008: 65).

7 Cited from Andre Pagliarini's translation of the passage of the order incorporated into a text by Bráz Hermenegildo do Amaral (see Williams et al., 2016: 41–44).

8 The Lazarette of Valongo was a place where all the sick Africans arriving in the port were to be quarantined.

9 The three slave traders were João Gomes Valle, Jose Luiz Alves and João Álvares de Souza Guimarães and Company (Honorato, 2008: 105; Pereira, 2007: 106).

10 Particularly revealing in this respect is the analysis carried out by Honorato (2006: 8) of the chief medical officer Vieira Silva's report on his difficulties in implementing the state health services before the opening of his lazarette: 'There were more than a few conflicts between the traders and Vieira Silva. On the other hand, the efficiency of the commissioner's office is questionable, given the financial difficulties and the scarce number of functionaries in handling the service. Additionally, it was nearly unanimous in travellers' logs that health and hygiene were neglected in Valongo and that its activities were nearly always characterised by great cruelty'.

11 The merit of Act 581 (Império do Brasil, 1850) was to make illegal not only the conduct of the slave trader, but of all of those involved in the trade chain. According to Art. 3: 'Anyone who imports or attempts importation, be he the owner, the captain or the master, the pilot or the boatswain of the vessel is guilty of an offense. The crew and those assisting the disembarkation of slaves on Brazilian territory, or those who attempt to conceal knowledge of such from the authorities or to circumvent apprehension at sea, or in the act of disembarkation being pursued, are guilty of complicity'.

4 From the first attempts at industrialisation to financialisation

'Little Africa' vs Porto Maravilha

A law of 1850 is extremely significant for the study of capitalist accumulation in Brazil: the Land Act. Proclaimed on 28 September 1850, the law ruled no less than the private ownership of land in Brazil. From the beginning of colonisation to the country's independence in 1822, a regime of *sesmarias* – or allotments – had prevailed, according to which the Portuguese Crown could grant the right to use the colony's land to whomever it wished in accordance with its objective to occupy and secure its borders. For their part, the allotters, just like brotherhoods and religious orders, could lease or grant the right to use land (already ceded by the Crown) to allottees in exchange for payment in the form of currency or a portion of the harvest. However, even after the cession and occupation by allotters, the Crown ultimately held the land. Given the prime objective of occupying the land and stimulating its productive use in order to generate tributes for the Crown, the mere occupation of land was not necessarily punished, as demonstrated by many cases where squatters were thanked, after having occupied the land, with the concession of an allotment (Fonseca, 2005: 106).

While the land was basically worked by African hands and their descendants within the slavery regime, the use and occupation of new (not yet occupied) lands did not require rigid inspection, nor were severe penalties or sanctions necessary for squatters. In the end, the supply of slaves allotted to the land and its respective master guaranteed production on the plantations. It was enough to impose punishment upon those who attempted to escape or who rebelled against their enslavement. Meanwhile, the prohibition of the slave trade and the transition towards wage labour in the agricultural-export economy called for the separation between potential wage labourers and the land, so that these would 'accept' the wage regime.

In agreement with this, the Land Act of 1850, together with the amendment which followed in 1854, came to fill the legal void opened by the end of the allotment regime following Brazil's independence. It established three clear criteria for the recognition of possession and transferral of the ownership of land that was lawfully cultivated and occupied. Land which did not comply with the stipulations of productive use was treated as public vacant land, that is, as state property, which could only be returned to private owners by means of sale. Any other form of occupation was subject to 'heavy penalties' (Fonseca, 2005: 108). At the same

58 *From industrialisation to financialisation*

time, the act established certain tasks for the state, including promoting immigration of free foreign labourers to Brazil in order to fill the labour demand on the exporting farms as well as other activities that could no longer rely on slave labour.

The Land Act established that the costs of financing the immigration enterprise as well as the vast administrative process involved in measuring and regulating the ownership of public and private lands was to be covered by the proceeds from the sale of public land. Due to its breadth, it appears that Fonseca (2005: 111–112) was right in concluding that the act and its different instruments represented a fundamental inflection of the notion of property in the country, despite historians' doubts concerning the capacity of the Brazilian state to enforce the law in the 19th century. After all, this act made available the land '(and also the labour-power) for a free, capitalist market' (Fonseca, 2005: 111–112).

Although the Land Act had a more direct effect on rural areas, it also had important consequences for the urban rearrangement of Rio de Janeiro. What is particularly relevant is the effect it had on the relationship between the Church and the state, seeing that during the colonial period, the 'religious orders with their property and agrarian holdings constituted a key vector of occupation in the cities' (Fridman, 1999: 235). At first, the Jesuits assumed the leading role in the organisation of housing. After they were expelled from the colony in 1759, the Benedictines came to play the central role in the housing sector. Like the Jesuits, they produced the building materials on their farms and supervised the work of the slaves. The latter constructed the houses which would later be leased to non-nobles, who were not granted their own allotments, had no other access to housing and were thus captive clients of the clergymen (Fridman, 1999: 235).

While creating a capitalist land market, the act also brought about a rapid fragmenting of lands both in central and in rural areas adjacent to the city, the latter of which would gradually become suburbs in the last decades of the 19th century and at the beginning of the 20th. In this way, the great stretches of land 'belonging to plantation owners and friars and entrusted to third parties … [passed into the hands of] anonymous societies and allotment agencies … the largest buyers of lands, in order to construct central mills with individual bank loans, or villas and small planting plots' (Fridman, 1999: 223).

Attempts at industrialisation

The end of the slave trade, the resulting liberation of capital accumulated by means of the trade and the attempt to diversify investments by those who profited from the export of primary products all propelled industrial activities beginning in the second half of the 19th century, above all in the region of Rio de Janeiro. Until the 1930s, the expansion of these activities was restricted to a relatively small group of sectors, in particular those devoted to the production of food and drink, fabrics and clothing, leather, and wood and metallurgy, this last one in response to the demand for agricultural tools. In other words, the industrial activities developed in the region of Rio de Janeiro – the country's main industrial hub

From industrialisation to financialisation 59

at the time – reflect the most general characteristics of the country's industrialisation process. However, until the global crisis initiated by the stock market crash in New York in 1929, industrialisation was an activity of lesser economic significance, subordinate to agricultural exports, the country's real economic motor (Leopoldi, 2000: 41 ff).

With the international crisis and the failure of the agricultural export model, difficulties arose in importing manufactured goods; at the same time, in domestic politics, the rural oligarchies that dominated the national scene lost their hegemony. This initiated a period of strong state intervention in the economy with the purpose of inducing the process which became known as *ISI*, import substitution industrialisation. Starting especially in the 1940s, this process brought about a broad expansion of industrial activities by diversifying the production of consumer goods, which increasingly came to include durable consumer goods, and impelling the production of capital goods. It also led to the creation of a range of mechanisms and institutions unique to the developmentalist state, including agencies specialising in the financing of industry, administration of industrial and sectorial policies, controlling monetary policy, etc. (Cano, 2015: 446f; Fonseca and Salomão, 2016).

These changes toward the development of industrial activities are reflected in the forms in which Rio de Janeiro's urban space was occupied. During the period of those first industrial impulses, which were restricted to more traditional sectors, the bulk of industrial industries were geared toward more central areas of Rio de Janeiro. Yet already in the 1950s, the increase in the concentration of companies as well as the growth in the size of industrial plants demanded the shift of activities towards the suburbs and other towns in the state of Rio de Janeiro. As Oliveira and Rodrigues (2009: 132 ff) show, the reduced importance of the city as an industrial centre only accelerated in the following decades. For this reason, they assert, in addition to shifting industrial activities to other towns in the state, at least three other processes are observable in each of the subsequent decades:

i) The policy of decentralising economic activities promoted by the military governments (1964–1985) with the intention, among others, of favouring regional oligarchies reduced the availability of investments in the south-central part of the country. Although this decentralisation 'had positive effects on São Paulo's industry', given its near monopoly over the industry of capital goods, it was disastrous for industrial activity in Rio de Janeiro (Oliveira and Rodrigues, 2009: 132).

ii) The 1980s were characterised by the debt crisis, which marked 'the beginning of the financialisation process in the Brazilian economy' (Oliveira and Rodrigues, 2009: 133). As is well known, after taking out loans in a climate of low international interest rates in the 1970s, many developing countries, Brazil included, were forced to amortise their contracted debts, which had augmented exponentially due to high interest rates in the 1980s. The pressure to generate a balance of payments surplus and settle these debts increasingly compromised the policy of import substitution industrialisation.

60 *From industrialisation to financialisation*

Further, governments increased domestic interest rates to obtain the funds needed to roll over the internal public debt, leading companies to give up on productive investments in favour of financial market investments, feeding financialisation.

iii) In the 1990s, the readjustment and fiscal austerity policies exacerbated the social consequences of the 1980s crisis. A shift also took place in the country's monetary policy. In the 1980s, the Brazilian currency was devalued to stimulate exports, limit imports, generate commercial surpluses and pay off the interest on the external debt. In the 1990s, however, the 'macroeconomic' adjustment embodied by the so-called *Plano Real* of 1994 prioritised limiting inflation by strengthening the national currency, the *real*. However, by cheapening and consequently stimulating imports, the appreciation of the *real* favoured the entry of manufacturers into the country; this created tough competition for the country's industry. Thus, began the so-called 'precocious deindustrialisation' of the Brazilian economy, a process which to this day has not been reversed. The strong currency and high interest rates also fuelled financialisation, 'appreciating fictitious capital to the detriment of productive capital, with the exacerbated profits of the financial system; increasing also private, but mainly public debt; [and] increasing the wealth of the *rentier* segment of society' (Cano, 2017: 282). These consequences are also true for the state of Rio de Janeiro, even though the advance of oil drilling in the Campos Basin, located to the north of the city of Rio de Janeiro, has led to some dynamism in the region's economy. Yet for the city of Rio de Janeiro, the end of the 1990s represent the end of a cycle in which the city that was once the core and motor of the country's nascent industrial activity started to take on other functions:

> After the federal bureaucracy left, the city of Rio de Janeiro reshaped its own weight in the state economy by reaffirming its function as a provider of modern services, while the *Baixada Fluminense* (Fluminense Lowland) would reinforce its legacy with the consolidation of metal-mechanical and petrochemical industries.
>
> (Oliveira and Rodrigues, 2009: 135)

Little Africa

The transformations observed in the forms of occupation and use of the port district accompany a more general shift in the new functions that the city has assumed as well as those that it has lost since the end of the 19th century. In the second half of the 19th century, the city was growing and becoming denser in areas removed from the port, while the port district was continually losing commercial value. This devaluation came to a head after the abolition of the slave trade, which brought with it the closure of the market and the cemetery. Along with economic deceleration, the zones adjacent to the port, particularly in the highest areas, the hills of Providência and Pinto, came to be occupied more and

From industrialisation to financialisation 61

more by emancipated and later free blacks. One significant occupation of these hills came with the arrival of the combatants from the War of Canudos, a conflict between the federal government and a messianic movement located in the interior of Bahia, in 1897.[1] When the federal government did not keep its promise to provide housing for the ex-combatants in Rio de Janeiro, they occupied the Hill of Providência and renamed it *Hill of Favela* in allusion to the hill next to the city of Canudos and the common shrub in the Bahian hinterlands called *faveleira*. Thus, the *favela* was born 'from which all others take their name' (Cardoso, 2015: 187).

With the abolition of slavery in 1888 and the subsequent significant influx of migrants mainly from the Northeast of Brazil, the port district began solidifying its position as a residential area for the poor who lived with precarious infrastructure and only basic sanitation.[2] Dubbed 'Little Africa' by the composer and visual artist Heitor dos Prazeres (1898–1966), the area became a centre of Afrodescendent population and culture, in particular beginning around the end of the 19th century (Moura, 1995).[3] After 1888, 'Little Africa', which had been occupied especially by freedmen during slavery, received hundreds of former slaves who became free after abolition. Accordingly, 'Little Africa' transformed into a dynamic space of production of Afro-Brazilian culture, though it was seen with disdain by the elite concerned with reproducing high European culture.

The hills surrounding the port district – with 'Little Africa', their nucleus of political and cultural articulation – remained the place where the main popular revolts of early 20th-century Brazil were sparked: the Vaccine Revolt and the Revolt of the Lash. The first embodied the resistance to the hygienist policies that led to the destruction of tenement houses and the continual endeavours to remove the poor and black population from the centre of the city (Chalhoub, 1996; Pereira, 2002). The second symbolised the struggle against slaveholding mentality which, persisting after abolition, was materialised in the corporal punishments practiced by the navy officials against black sailors (Nascimento, 2008). These revolts were accompanied and followed by the struggles of stevedores and various movements in favour of the protection of Afrodescendent culture.

Indeed, the hills adjacent to the port district became a space of sociability, coexistence and resistance of the poor and black population (Moura, 1995: 69 ff). In this space, they lived in hovels, tenement houses and favelas' shanties, worked on loading and unloading ships, professed their customs, dances and religion and met in stage workers' associations. This ambience expressed the link between practices of Afrodescendent culture, the workplace and the political organisation of the residents. In this way, the houses of religious worship simultaneously served as residence for stevedores and venues for fetes. Similarly, important workers' associations like the *Sociedade de Resistência dos Trabalhadores em Trapiches de Café* (Society of Workers' Resistance in Coffee Piers), largely comprising blacks, supported the first Carnival associations.

It is in this physical space and cultural environment that manifestations such as *capoeira*, *Candomblé* and Afro-Brazilian rhythms were cultivated and transformed. It is also here that samba itself, combining rhythm, lyrics and dance, was born. Tia Ciata (Aunt Ciata) or Ciata de Oxum was one of the main

62 *From industrialisation to financialisation*

protagonists of this movement. Tia Ciata, the pseudonym with which Hilária Batista de Almeida became famous, was a cook, candomblé preacher and cultural activist who was born in 1854 in Santo Amaro da Purificação in Bahia and died in 1924 in Rio de Janeiro. After migrating to Rio de Janeiro, fleeing religious persecution in Bahia, she began organising around her home what would become a relevant nucleus of the Afro-Brazilian cultural manifestations (Moura, 1995).

Although this part of the city was stigmatised as violent and 'uncivilised', it was here that cultural repertoires evolved which, in the course of the 20th century, would become the most famous face of Brazil worldwide, as Cardoso (2015) exemplifies in the case of Carnival:

> The period between the 1910s and 1930s is remembered for the birth of modern carnival in Rio de Janeiro. During those decades, such canonical names such as Donga, João da Baiana, Sinhô, Heitor dos Prazeres und Pixinguinha all hung out in Saúde and Gamboa, and later Onze Square.[4]

Nevertheless, from the point of view of capital accumulation, at the turn of the 20th century, the space adjacent to the port was already sufficiently delinked from the market to construct a supply of assets which could be (re)integrated into the processes of production of value. It was at this time that the port district went through a new phase of capital expansion required by the global demands of industrial capital. As such, the public interventions promoted by the President of the Republic, Rodrigues Alves, and the mayor of Rio de Janeiro, Pereira Passos, were fundamental.

Rodrigues Alves and the modernisation of the port

The reforms promoted by Rodrigues Alves, president of Brazil from 1902 to 1906, sought to modernise port services and expand its capacity to export commodities so as to facilitate the entry of industrialised products from Europe and the USA as well as attract foreign labourers to work on coffee farms following the end of slavery (Pinheiro and Rabha, 2004: 65).

The federal projects in the port developed during the Alves government responded to the international tendency to substitute human manual labour with cranes and steam-powered machines, as had been pioneered in the port of London and later in the port of Buenos Aires. Various reforms were carried out, among them, the construction of a 3,500-metre-long pier and 18 warehouses (Soares and Moreira, 2007: 105; Vassalo, 2015: 63). To accomplish this, 10 beaches disappeared of which, today, only the names remain: Prainha, Saúde, Chichorra, Gamboa, Valongo, Formosa, Palmeiras, Lázaros, São Cristóvão and Caju. The pier was expanded in stages and the final construction, though still in progress, was inaugurated in 1910 under President Nilo Peçanha (Pinheiro and Rabha, 2004: 65). In the course of these reforms, entrusted to the English construction company C.H. Walker & Co Ltd, many houses in the area of the old Valongo

From industrialisation to financialisation 63

were demolished, forcing their residents, many of them former slaves who had migrated from Bahia, to the district of Cidade Nova (Figueiredo, 2005: 185).

The reforms in the port served to revitalise the functions of the port for global capital accumulation not only according to its activities-ends as a port of entry and exit of goods destined for the world market, but also its activity-means in the form of services of embarkation and disembarkation carried out in the port. It is equally relevant that Rio de Janeiro, from this point on, was definitively integrated into the global tourist market seeing as the port, with its new installations, became a common stopping point for the large cruise ships that visited Latin America (Figueiredo, 2005: 188).

The Pereira Passos reform

The urban reform of Rio de Janeiro was initiated by engineer Pereira Passos, who was commissioned mayor by Rodrigues Alves for the period of 1902–1906. It was in a way complementary and functional to the modernisation projects in the port, since the crux of the reform was to open large routes linking the port district to the rest of the districts in the city, thus facilitating the arrival and departure of products from the port to the interior of the city and the country. The new routes also followed the logic of the organic city, integrated not only in the sense that the port and commerce in the central areas were interlinked, but also that the areas experiencing expansion to the south (Botafogo, Copacabana, etc.) and in the suburbs (Meier, Engenho Novo, etc.) found rapid access to the city centre, the motor of 'civilisation' with its theatres and colleges.

Inspired by the renewal of Paris directed by mayor Georges-Eugène Haussmann between 1853 and 1870, Pereira Passos sought to complete the work of the federal government in its modernising ideology by driving out both colonial hallmarks and, in his judgement, the relics from the past that still marked the centre of Rio de Janeiro. In addition to the specific programme of urban renewal, Pereira Passos initiated a hygienist and disciplinary policy, which penalised behaviours considered incompatible with the modern city. This included prohibiting religious practices linked to candomblé and punishing manifestations linked to Afrodescendent music and dance. As seen, this occurred at exactly the same time as the precursors of samba were beginning to develop in so-called 'Little Africa'. In his eagerness to modernise the old colonial capital, Pereira Passos was the boldest bearer and operator of the programme to imitate Europe, eliminating and repressing any expression of popular local culture contrary to his civilising ideal:

> In the attempt to impose 'civility' on the inhabitants of the city, in the course of his tenure Pereira Passos emitted a series of prohibitions related to urban practices common in the city: He prohibited spitting in the street and in trams, canine vagrancy, building fires in city streets, releasing balloons, peddling lottery tickets, displaying meat for sale in the streets, milking cows in the city as well as walking around the streets without shoes and a shirt. With these restrictions, Pereira Passos sought to substitute old urban practices with

64   *From industrialisation to financialisation*

new habits he deemed 'civilised'. What is more, the mayor prohibited the *Entrudo*, substituting it with flower battles and tore down the kiosks in the centre of the city, in this way stimulating the opening of shops selling afternoon tea.[5]

(Azevedo, 2003: 62–63)

Furthermore, the Pereira Passos Reform renewed hundreds of buildings and brought about monumental infrastructure projects with the intention of valorising the south-central zone of the city, forcing the poorest segment of the population to move to the suburbs, find accommodation in simple housing around the port or occupy the hills adjacent to it. Thus, in the context of urban renewal, this reform envisioned that Rio de Janeiro would adopt 'high Western culture' as a model and revalorise its real estate and territory in the centre by imposing sanitary and urbanistic measures presented as the very materialisation of the European civilisatory ideal.

For our interests, namely, nexuses with capital accumulation, the urban reform promoted by Pereira Passos generally reinforced the effects unleashed by the 'technological modernisation' propagated by Rodrigues Alves. On the one hand, both reforms followed a repressive logic against the local population, whose political organisations, stevedore unions and black culture were severely criminalised, considered obstacles to the expansion of accumulation and the imaginary of civilisation. The action of the state in the area was therefore limited to the disciplinary aspect: it prohibited the organisation of port workers, religious practices, music and dance. This whole process brought about the expulsion of the old residents in the name of beautifying the area and modernising the port.

On the other hand, the reforms facilitated transport between the port district and the city and optimised the functioning of the port as a link between Brazil and the global economy. This led to the maximisation of gains from the port services, which were granted (after the considerable public revamping of the port by the federal government) to the private concessionaire Daniel Henninger & Damart & Comp. 'that later ceded its rights by means of transferral to Compagnie du Port de Rio de Janeiro' (Pinheiro and Rabha, 2004: 71).

With regard to the land contiguous to the port, the two reforms promoted a transformation both of the flat areas (partially expanded by landfills and demolitions) and the adjacent hills. The flat areas, which belonged to the federal government, came to be occupied by warehouses and public repartitions, and therefore remained 'voids' which were to be occupied in future reforms (Pinheiro and Rabha, 2004: 68). The hills, in turn, were occupied more and more by the poor population, which consisted both of persons evicted from tenement houses demolished by Pereira Passos in the city centre and of those who had newly migrated to the city. In any case, these were urban territories that were not a part of the real estate market proper, where the most important sums were circulating, and although they had some value for trade, they were located outside of the circuit of capitalist accumulation.

From industrialisation to financialisation 65

The decommodification of the port district in the 20th century

Generally speaking, one could say that the port district went through a process of disconnection from the dynamic core of capitalist accumulation, and the port, in its activities-ends and -means, would lose its relevance for the process of accumulation decades later. In the course of the 20th century, the developmentalist policy in its emphasis on import substitution industrialisation demanded another type of port structure capable of handling growing volumes of both imports of capital goods as well as exports of prime materials and agricultural products (which continued to be the main exports). Traditional ports in central areas, like the one in Rio de Janeiro, saw their expansion capacity hampered by the new urban functions and designs. Instead, new city-ports emerged which, located next to industrial parks, practically became an extension of the assembly line, enabling rapid movement between import, production and export. Hence, the city's port ceded its place of importance to other Brazilian ports.

In the same way that Rio's port became less attractive for capitalist investment for no longer serving as a link between the Brazilian and global economies and a space of value production for the port services, its surroundings experienced a long phase of devaluation. The area thus came into the 1990s as a 'precarious and degraded' space, and the authorities even attempted to expunge the vitality of its existing political–cultural production.

One century after the renovation of the port and Pereira Passos' urban reform, a situation took shape which, from the perspective of capital accumulation, was quite different from that observed at the threshold of the 20th century. That is, from the point of view of its activity-ends (embarkation and disembarkation of goods) and port services, Rio de Janeiro's port – which was the principal Brazilian port at the beginning of the 20th century – is of little relevance today. It has dropped to eighth place in the movement of cargo, also suffering from the direct competition of the more modern port of Itaguaí, created in 1982 and situated just 100 km to the south. In 2016, the port operated a cargo volume that did not even represent 10% of the volume moved by the port of Santos, the country's largest port (ABRAETEC, 2016). Furthermore, port activities were shifted to the north to the district of Caju.

In contrast, the urban territory in the areas neighbouring the old port are once again being integrated in the dynamic of accumulation. This tendency is a recent one, and it represents to some extent a reaction to the problems created by the type of privileged urbanisation which took place in the last decades of the 20th century. The move of the capital to Brasília in 1960, taking away a large number of public offices and functionaries priorly installed in the centre of Rio de Janeiro, and the growing tendency of the wealthy to move to the southern part of town rendered the centre less and less important. In this context, it is also worth highlighting the role played by the growth of the city towards the new neighbourhood 'Barra da Tijuca', in the east of the city, after the 1970s. As Moreira (2003: 82) shows:

> The new neighbourhood would have been a new centre, capable of offering a high quality of life to its inhabitants which, according to the ideals of the

66 *From industrialisation to financialisation*

time, meant a clean view, insulation, ventilation, easy circulation and the specialisation of functions, in addition to security, infrastructure, commerce and services.

In sum, a model of urbanity is being implemented which is clearly inspired by cities like Miami, founded in the social homogeneity of the wealthy upper middle classes in a coastal district distant from the centre. The homogeneity is only disrupted by the 'temporary presence of domestic workers and employees of local commerce'. Urbanistically, the model adopted is that of the 'dispersion of nuclei erected on the territory, interlinked by roads and linked to the rest of the city by motorways' (Moreira, 2003: 84).

The Porto Maravilha project

In recent decades, the urbanistic model described above has started exhibiting clear signs of exhaustion. The number of automobiles multiplied, congesting the motorways, and the segregated social spaces started exhibiting diverse fractures as a consequence of social dislocations produced by progressive policies adopted during the period 2003–2015 at the federal level.

In this context, the dynamic real estate market of Rio de Janeiro changed. There has been renewed interest in real estate in the centre, providing evidence that the old port district can be reintegrated into capitalist accumulation as a space offering residence and services to wealthier social groups, as shown by Andreatta and Herce (2011: 137):

> It might seem anecdotal, but in the year 2005 a property developer in Riachuelo Street, approximately one kilometre from the area of the port (the first sale in 20 years in the centre), sold its 688 apartments in less than two hours! This proves the existence of a residential demand in the centre which has begun to transform the paradigm of the real estate market that until now considered operations in the space of housing for middle classes economically unviable. This was an important and symbolic event, and many real estate operators who up to now were only active in the southern part of the city have begun to seek territory and real estate in the centre, in the port district, and in the adjacent neighbourhood of São Cristóvão.

The new interest that developers have shown in the port district has served as a precondition for reconnecting the zone to capitalist accumulation. The reasons for this interest vary. One of them is the rediscovery of local cultural manifestations by the rich youth who live in the southern part of the city and use the port area more and more as their leisure space. The perspectives of hosting the 2014 World Cup and 2016 Olympics were also important because they highlighted the tourist potential of 'revitalising' the city's historical centre. It is equally important that there was accumulated dissatisfaction with the model of urbanisation which led the wealthy population to live in gated communities in areas very far away from

From industrialisation to financialisation 67

the city centre. This created the favourable context for investment in real estate and stimulated the implementation of a new programme of urban restructuring of all of the port district, the Porto Maravilha project, conceived in 2009.

This project, as we have seen, envisages the intervention in an area of 5 million square metres and 70 kilometres of roads and expressways. This area is located in the centre of the city and encompasses the historical neighbourhoods of Santo Cristo, Gamboa and Saúde, as well as parts of Centro, Caju, Cidade Nova and São Cristóvão. According to projections, the project's implementation will cause the area's population, estimated at 32,000 inhabitants, to swell to 100,000 inhabitants within 10 years (Porto Maravilha, 2011).

This project initially followed the global tendency of dispossession of cities in the context of financial capitalism, i.e., the gentrified revitalisation of historical centres and in particular port areas, as well as the use of sporting mega-events to restructure the urban space in order to create value (Harvey, 2002). Various studies have pointed to the importance of these mega-events in including cities in new financial flows (Burbank et al., 2001; Gaffney, 2010; Roche, 2000; Soares, 2013; Whitson and Horne, 2006). This is because they impel a series of programmes to restructure the host cities in order to boost mass international tourism, erect a new set of buildings, add value to the ground and attract real estate investments. According to Gaffney (2010: 27), mega-events impose a 'neo-liberal shock doctrine' to accelerate the commodification of cities. In recent cases, the mega-events were always associated with revamping old, devalued central areas for accumulation by means of public and private investments, as is the case of Rio's port (Soares, 2013: 200).

Harvey (2002: 104 ff) shows that this pattern of accumulation has followed the example of Barcelona, where the 1992 Olympic Games created major opportunities for the accumulation of monopoly rents. This accumulation appropriated Catalonian symbolic and cultural capital to 'sell' the image and the areas of the city on the global market. It contributed to transform the city's architecture, urban fabric and local commerce with the opening of large enterprises (museums, venues, etc.). Yet this process was marked by various contradictions. If it is true that the 'irresistible lure' of Catalonian culture 'draws more and more homogenizing multinational commodification in its wake', it is no less true that the reforms in Barcelona removed the poor population, appropriated public areas, eliminated local commerce, etc. (Harvey, 2002: 104–105).

On that note, in the port area of Rio de Janeiro, more specifically in the Hill of Providência, the city's oldest favela, many tenants were displaced to make room for constructions needed for the Olympics (Rainha and Fonseca, 2013). It is not only that these displacements highlight the connection between the sporting mega-events and this new stage of accumulation in the port district. Mayor Eduardo Paes himself also stressed the importance of the Olympics in propelling the Porto Maravilha project. Indeed, the 'Olympic Boulevard', created on the grounds of the Porto Maravilha project, combined all the possibilities for accumulation opened up by sporting mega-events, as the programme of inauguration of the Boulevard in August 2016 shows. Among its many cultural and

68   *From industrialisation to financialisation*

culinary attractions, the programme included the Coca Cola Parade, the Samsung Galaxy Studio, a bungee jump sponsored by Nissan, the travelling exhibit 'Se Prepara Brasil' (Prepare yourself, Brazil) sponsored by the insurance company Bradesco Seguros, the Skol (a brewery) Panoramic Balloon and a Nike shop (Porto Maravilha, 2016).

The process of implementing the Porto Maravilha project and negotiations with the local population imposed some adjustments on the plan, especially with regard to the tension between urban reform and the preservation of the architectural, archaeological and cultural heritage of the area. According to Vassallo (2015: 65), from the very first moment of its implementation, the project clearly followed a discourse grounded in 'terms such as "empty", "isolation" and "degradation" which justify its revitalisation and modernisation', as seen in ex-mayor Paes' declaration, cited in the introduction. The creation of two large museums – the MAR, Art Museum Rio de Janeiro, and the *Museu do Amanhã* (Museum of Tomorrow) – indicate in a way the wish to reform and fill this supposedly 'empty' and 'degraded' space represented by the port district, not only from a concrete point of view but also a symbolic one.

It is true that, in their implementation, both museums had to establish some sort of negotiation with the local culture. Nevertheless, the modernist icons and the praise of the future, mainly materialised in the Museum of Tomorrow (2015), 'conceived and realised in collaboration with the Roberto Marinho Foundation, an institution linked to the Globo Group, with the bank Santander as its main sponsor and Shell as a cosponsor … and with Engie, IBM and IRB Brasil Resseguros as sponsors', represent a clear rupture with what the district used to represent.

The public hearings and the clashes with the local population, in addition to the archaeological excavations that pointed to the existence of the above analysed Cemetery of Pretos Novos, the Valongo Wharf and the Imperatriz Wharf, highlight the lacunas in the discourse of emptiness and isolation. The inclusion of local cultural producers (musicians, artisans, *capoeira* artists, etc.) in certain cultural projects developed in the area of the port, in accordance with the law from 2009 which stipulates the directives of the project, also contributed to showing the implausibility of the discourses that seek to construe the area as empty and in need of civilisation and occupation.

Equally relevant in this process were the various resistance movements that have formed against the project. Alluding explicitly to the legacy of the mobilisations of 'Little Africa', this resistance has sought to strengthen the link between culture, labour and politics, expressing it in collective actions of production of public spaces. Consonant with this orientation, the squares and streets of the area are regularly occupied by samba circles (*Roda da Pedra do Sal, Samba da Lei, Samba Honesto*) and carnival blocks (*Cordão do prata preta, Fala meu louro, Bloco pinto sarado*) which, in spite of the presence of frequenters from wealthier classes, are free and combine different social groups in an open atmosphere. In the Hill of Providência and Hill of Conceição, cultural collectives such as the *Instituto Favelarte* and the *Projeto Mauá* have become focal points for the dissemination of local artists. Moreover, the port district has experienced diverse

From industrialisation to financialisation 69

collective occupations of abandoned buildings such as the occupations *Quilombo das Guerreiras, Chiquinha Gonzaga, Zumbi dos Palmares, Flor do Asfalto* and *Machado de Assis*. Based on another perception of the city, all of these political actions have to a greater or lesser extent challenged the different phases and interventions of the Porto Maravilha project. The mentioned recognition of the area as a World Heritage Site in July of 2017 represents an extraordinary strengthening of the position of those collectives who oppose the project's erasure of the past.

In the face of these confrontations, many forms of entangled accumulation have taken place in the port district in the context of the Porto Maravilha project. Mechanisms of accumulation by dispossession persist, particularly in the case of residents who occupy buildings without an adequate title deed:

> The occupations Zumbi dos Palmares, Flor do Asfalto and Machado de Assis were evicted because of the Urban Project Porto Maravilha, a project which seeks to 'revitalise' the port district of Rio de Janeiro, whose realisation presupposes the substitution of the poor resident stratum with more adequate strata of economic and urban hegemonic objectives.
>
> (Assumpção and Schramm, 2013: 97, 98)

However, the most obvious form of accumulation – the association between the state and financial capital to create new spaces of accumulation – is typical of financialised capitalism.

The financial engineering of Porto Maravilha

In order to execute the Porto Maravilha project, the Municipal Law No. 101/2009 established the 'Special Area of Urbanistic Interest' as well as the Company of Urban Development of the Port Region of Rio de Janeiro (CDURP), a semi-public society with the City Hall of Rio de Janeiro as its majority shareholder, responsible for implementing the works and generating the assets and financial resources for the project. To finance the infrastructure projects and the construction of the buildings in the zone, an ingenious public–private partnership was created. To mobilise the resources needed to develop the works, the Real Estate Investment Fund of the Port Region (FIIP) was created, whose assets are the land where construction was to take place, as well as *Certificates of Additional Construction Potential* (CEPAC). CEPACs are securities granted by the City Hall, negotiated on the stock exchange and linked to conditional fundraising; in other words, the CDURP can only invest funds raised in works planned in the port district. In contrast, the title buyers acquire 'the right to build beyond the normal limits in areas which will receive extended infrastructure' (BM&FBOVESPA, 2015). An important aspect of this is the fiscal and administrative facilities offered by the municipality to the investor:

> Another element of this model is the legal establishment of fiscal incentives. As part of the model, fiscal incentives that include discounts and exemptions

70 *From industrialisation to financialisation*

of municipal taxes are offered to enterprises founded in the first years of the operation. Also, procedures for project approval were accelerated in the City Hall.

(Arraes and Silva, 2014)

The right to execute the infrastructure projects and urban services was granted to the consortium Porto Novo, made up of three construction companies: on the one hand, Odebrecht and OAS (each with the participation of 37.5%), and on the other, Carioca (with the participation of 25%) (Porto Novo, 2010).[6]

As far as real estate is concerned, the project *initially* proved successful. Starting in 2011, the entire port district experienced intense financial appreciation. According to the Association of Real Estate Managers of Rio de Janeiro (ADEMIRJ), expectations linked to the Porto Maravilha project increased the area's price per square metre by 300% (ADEMIRJ, 2012). Even the sale of the CEPACs followed a sort of road map. In June 2011, the CEF (Federal Savings Bank), using resources from the Brazilian workers' social security fund, the *Fundo de Garantia do Tempo de Serviço* (FGTS), acquired a minimum value of 3.5 billion BRL (US\$ 0.9 billion as of 29 June 2018) by auctioning all offered CEPACs as a bundled unit. To garner the rest of the funds necessary to carry out the planned projects for an estimated value of 8 billion BRL (US\$ 2,07 billion as of 29 June 2018), the CDURP bet on the regularisation of land and the sale of lots in the area. The CEF, for its part, expected to resell the titles or negotiate the titles with construction companies, receiving real estate units in the region (Cardoso, 2013: 75 ff; Nogueira, 2011). The ex-mayor Eduardo Paes celebrated the success of the auction:

The thing I am most sure about is the transformative power of this public–private partnership.

(O Globo, 2011)

However, the mayor's comment does not reveal that this was a quite *sui generis* public–private partnership. After all, the purchaser of the title was a public bank using funds belonging to Brazilian workers (Cardoso, 2013: 80). Indeed, the dynamic of the Porto Maravilha project confirms one of the tendencies of financial capitalism: the use of workers' provisions and guarantees for speculative ends. In other words, it is a mechanism of transferring risks and wagers to popular classes, who find themselves in a situation of inequality in financial operations – and, indeed, outside of it entirely (Soederberg, 2013).

In 2012, the climate was still one of euphoria among the executives of the state bank CEF that celebrated the doubling of the unit value of the CEPACs (Porto Maravilha, 2013). Yet from 2015 on, the project has suffered a series of setbacks. On the one hand, Brazil's extended economic crisis fully shattered the expectations of profit attached to the undertaking, thus curtailing the appreciation of the region's real estate. In this context, the difficulties of financing the works and

From industrialisation to financialisation 71

services became apparent, leading to the partial suspension of activities between July and November 2017 due to the failure of the government to pay the concessionaire Porto Novo.[7] Correspondingly, the titles acquired by the State bank CEF ran aground. By November 2017, the bank had only managed to sell 8% of the titles it had bought. Private investors' interest in the titles and in the area had hit rock bottom (O Globo, 2017).

On the other hand, the investigations carried out by the Federal Public Ministry into the 'Car Wash Operation' showed that some of the protagonists of the programme of urban reform were involved in corruption.[8] The three construction companies responsible for the execution of the works, Odebrecht, OAS and Carioca, have all been indicted and have even had directors sentenced and indeed imprisoned recently. The sponsors of the Carioca construction company confessed that the Porto Novo consortium paid 52 million BRL (US$ 13.5 million as of 29 June 2018) to the then President of Chamber of Deputies, Eduardo Cunha (currently in prison) in exchange for his support in the negotiations, which freed up FGTS resources for investments in the port district (Carta Capital, 2016).

Besides these accusations, the Internet activist network Meu Rio (My Rio) has pressured city councillors to create a CPI (parliamentary committee of enquiry), which ascertained at least five other alleged irregularities in the Porto Maravilha project, including the misappropriation of funds by the CDURB, the sale of public land under market value to the FIIPM, noncompliance with a law that stipulates the provision of land for the construction of council housing, noncompliance with environmental laws and *post factum* contract changes that restrict the social benefits of the project (CPI do Porto Maravilha, 2017).

Note that these practices of expropriation are revamped in the context of financial capitalism. The movement observed here is two-fold. Firstly, on the discursive-symbolic level and the level of the urban dynamic itself, an area emerges that is central in geographical terms, but peripheral as far as accumulation is concerned; it is a demographic vacuum, isolated from the capitalist city. At the same time, the capitalist occupation of this exterior, which has not yet been integrated into accumulation, demands that infrastructure investments be carried out with resources given by investors who in fact will be the only ones able to appropriate the new value created in the space to be reoccupied. The CEPACs materialise this double movement of entangled accumulation because they allow the state to remodel the non-commodified space to integrate it into the process of accumulation. At the same time, the CEPACs guarantee the monopoly over the exploitation of the new space of accumulation to a select group of investors previously defined.

It is ironic that, today, the titles are property of the FGTS and are being administered by a public bank. If the current falling trend changes and titles start being sold, the fund will end up stronger. Selling them at a profit, however, implies new projects and the removal of the poor and working population in the area. If those titles are not sold and the works in the area do not continue, there will likely be

72　*From industrialisation to financialisation*

no removals, yet this would entail colossal financial losses for the workers' social security fund. This will be discussed in detail in the next chapter.

The contradictory role of culture

Culture plays an ambivalent role in this process. On the one hand, the museums and cultural programmes created in the area as well as the emphasis on 'economic exploitation of material and immaterial cultural heritage' (Porto Maravilha, n.d.) seek to augment the value of the space that is symbolically and physically being recreated:

> Porto Maravilha thus follows the tendency of revitalisation projects in various countries to try to attract a middle and upper-class clientele and develop tourism in hitherto worker neighbourhoods.
>
> (Vassallo, 2015: 67)

Yet, at the same time, the emphasis placed on culture in a district marked by a long history of independent cultural production creates new political opportunities for the local population to resist attempts to merely instrumentalise its local cultural manifestations for the purpose of aggregating symbolic value to the new territory of capital accumulation. That is, the stylisation of local cultural movements as territories of authenticity and tradition not yet penetrated by capitalist accumulation creates opportunities for subjects to articulate their resistance to the use of their production and their memory as mechanisms of capital valorisation for the benefit of big investors.

We can surmise from the work of Vassallo (2015) that the clashes between the movements of cultural resistance and the public–private partnership in favour of entangled accumulation do not yet have a clear victor. Perhaps it is possible that producers of culture will maintain the autonomy of production and commercialisation of their cultural goods; yet it is equally possible that they will be fully incorporated into Porto Maravilha as simple service providers to the real estate and leisure enterprises that have dominated new spaces of capitalist accumulation created in the port district.

Yet some tendencies and developments in this ongoing confrontation can be observed. On the one hand, the public–private partnership established for the Porto Maravilha project seems to have permanently redefined its discursive strategies. As opposed to classical modernisation discourses adopted when the project first surfaced, according to which an urban vacuum should be filled with progress and meaning, the current emphasis lies on the contribution the project is making to recuperating the history and memory of the area. The case of excavations in the area of the Cais do Valongo is emblematic. At first seen by the municipality of Rio de Janeiro primarily as a problem and obstacle for keeping the envisioned projects on schedule, as the archaeologists responsible for the excavations have implied (Lima et al., 2016: 317–318), the discoveries made there and the possibility that the site could be recognised as a World Heritage Site, as it indeed was in 2017,

From industrialisation to financialisation 73

provoked a major change of course on the part of the administrators. Now, these administrators view the Porto Maravilha project as openly pursuing the objective of uncovering the area's historical heritage, as clearly demonstrated in this article written by the president of the CDUR:

> The Valongo/Imperatriz Wharf represents a synthesis both of the process of transformation and the wealth of this new place in construction. Apart from the archaeological findings in themselves, from the urbanistic, histori- cal, political and symbolical point of view, the incorporation of the pier as an open-air memorial to the Jornal do Comércio Square is a milestone – not because it is the first such case, but because of what it represents for Porto Maravilha, for the city and for history.
>
> (Silva, 2015)

The other important tendency consolidated here is the formation of coalitions and networks among various mobilisations and organisations that have critically accompanied the development of the project. The campaign spearheaded by the group Meu Rio to create a CPI to investigate the Porto Maravilha project is one of the examples of such networks. The Community Forum of the Port, comprised of universities, collectives and parliamentarians, is another important actor. It struc- tures its actions around struggles against the policies of unequal development in the port district, expropriations of land and housing and the privatisations of public space and in this way seeks to confront the exclusive and entrepreneurial model of the city represented by the project. All of these mobilisations are an alternative to this new phase of seizure of the port district by capitalist accumula- tion. Their emergence shows that a tragic history can take unexpected turns, even if it stubbornly repeats itself in the form of a farce.

Notes

1 The War of Canudos was a rebellion conducted by the inhabitants of the small village of Canudos in the backlands of Bahia, led by the 'lay prophet' Antonio Conselheiro against the military forces of the Brazilian federal government in the period 1896– 1897. The messianic rebellion ended, '[a]fter three failed government expeditions [...], with the destruction of the community and the deaths of most of its inhabitants'. The conflict was made universally known by the book by Euclides da Cunha, *Rebellion in the Backlands*, originally published in 1902 (Johnson, 2000:3).
2 The commercial uses of the areas adjacent to the port also changed, hosting activities considered less noble such as sex work for clients with weak purchasing power: 'com- mercial sex was geographically segregated by class and race: cheap street prostitution, chiefly offered by women of color, was concentrated in Sacramento parish, north and west of the docks. On the other end of the social spectrum, the multiracial prostitutes who serviced an elite clientele enjoyed certain freedoms of movement among the city's bordellos, cabarets, and private homes'. (Williams et al., 2016: 130)
3 'Little Africa', according to Moura (1995: 92) extended from the area of the pier to the Cidade Nova and had its *capital* in the Onze Square.
4 The reference to 'modern Carnival' here is fundamental for distinguishing the carnival which was popularised in the 20th century and born in the so-called carnivalesque

74 *From industrialisation to financialisation*

parades of the port district from the carnival involving masks brought from Venice into elite Rio parlours in the second half of the 19th century. As Alencastro (1997: 52) shows, starting in the 1840s, 'in the largest most public dances, a fundamental rupture was occurring. The street celebrations, popular and black yet of Portuguese origin – the *Entrudo* – split from the white and segregated parlour Carnival'.

5 *Entrudo* was a popular celebration that took place in the three days preceding the beginning of Lent. This celebration was characterised by the mutual release of water and other liquids. In its place, Pereira Passos proposed another type of celebration in which people threw each other fragrant and colourful petals of flowers. (Alencastro, 1997: 52; Costa, 2000: 55).

6 For a detailed analysis of the financial modeling of the Porto Maravilha project, see Cardoso (2013). For a research of the patterns of urban regulation that emerged in the respective project, see Pereira (2015).

7 A note from the concessionaire communicates that, due to failed payment, 'The services of preservation and maintenance of the road system, green spaces and squares, public and pavement lighting, drainage systems, urban real estate, historical monuments and tourist destinations and transport signal systems (signs and street lights, for example), and works dedicated to maintaining and constructing new infrastructure, in addition to the collection of domestic rubbish and urban sanitation, will be suspended starting on 5 July, as stipulated in the contract' (Porto Novo, 2017a). Another note, from 15 November 2017, informs of the reinstatement of these services (Porto Novo, 2017b).

8 *Car Wash Operation* is a set of ongoing investigations and denunciations which seek to ascertain corruption schemes between public actors and entrepreneurs of large companies, developed mainly in the governments of the Workers' Party (2003–2016). (see Watts, 2017)

5 Crisis anchored at the port

The port's landscape has changed significantly since the end of the 2016 Olympics. Together, the icons of the mega project Porto Maravilha, the *Museum of Tomorrow*, the boulevard and the large towers, are all at the same time, an image of both abandonment and stagnation. Empty properties, the accumulation of trash, paralyzed construction sites and deteriorating squares and gardens, all comprise the scene for those who visit or live in the region (O Globo, 2018a). There is the general feeling, and above all in the areas where the largest real estate developments were constructed, that there is a large demographic and economic void. Regardless of the urban renovation and the intense flows of valorisation, the space appears to have entered a (new) phase of decommodification.

The scene described above, one that is profoundly contradictory, could better serve as an example of the contrasts that characterise what the late supporters of the modernisation theory call the 'peripheral modernity' or also a confirmation that, in 'backward' countries, projects are always interrupted by poor management, inefficiency or conflicts of interests. In this sense, it would not be surprising that even gentrification – defended in 2015 by the former mayor Paes discussing Porto Maravilha based on his understanding of urban interventions in London, New York or Berlin – could not be accomplished in the area where the largest consortium of urban reforms in Rio de Janeiro or in Brazil has operated (*Jornal do Brasil*, 2017a).

Although questions of collision or convergence of interests between actors and local capital that comprise the urban governance are important to understand the success or failure of large urban projects, they also cannot be analysed in a way that is disconnected from the global circuits of production and circulation of value. The Porto Maravilha has been profoundly affected by the economic, political and social crises that have crossed global capitalism since 2007 and reached Brazil most starkly starting in 2014. In the last four years, the situation has been continuously becoming worse. With the downturn of the real estate market, there are no buyers for the overvalued CEPACs, which authorise the construction of buildings higher than that the legislation allows. With that, the public–private partnership cannot be implemented and the payment services to the Concessionaire Porto Novo, which administers the area, is not fulfilled (Werneck et al., 2018: 6–7; Pública, 2018). The image and feeling are of a complete abandonment of the area.

76 *Crisis anchored at the port*

It is clear that the crisis that is anchored at the port is not isolated. And that obviously refers less to the fact that in the situation it is possible to find elements of the global economic crisis – like, for example, the overaccumulation of finance capital, oscillations in the real estate market, speculation, financialisation of workers subsistence funds, etc. – and much more because the diverse contemporary crises are connected and intertwined. In the case of the current finance-led capitalist accumulation, it is not possible to talk about the autonomy of domestic economies. At the same time, as they are stimulated by credit bubbles and monetary policies based on the purchasing of government bonds and/or the emission of paper securities, which flood the market with excess money, the liberalisation of these domestic economies to the transnational finance flows makes them more and more dependent on, and sensitive to, the oscillations of the global market.

In that sense, pulled by the exit of foreign capital after the *Lehman Brother* crisis, and by the worsening of the international economic scenario due to the Euro crisis, the weak recovery of the United States and the deceleration of the Chinese economy (that impacts Brazilian commodity-based exports portfolio), Brazil entered an extreme recession with an accumulated fall of 7.2% of the GDP in the two years of 2015 and 2016 (the worse since 1948, when the Brazilian Institute of Geography and Statistics started monitoring economic growth) and high rates of unemployment (De Paula and Pires, 2017: 127 ff.). Political instability and protests, like those that have already erupted in Greece, Portugal and Spain in recent years, became the norm.

The Brazilian economic recession reached its most radical expression in the State of Rio de Janeiro, where it became popular to say that the 'the country's crisis' was 'felt in the skin'. To use Lessa's metaphor (2000), Rio turned into the 'mirror of the nation'. Indeed, it already was, according to the author. For him, the region that housed the country's most longstanding capital and is the birthplace of coffee plantations, which then expanded territorially and was iconic for the Republic's wealth, became a synthesis of Brazil. It forged a society without any regional interests that participated very little in the federal tensions and was not even capable of turning into a bureaucratic centre after the end of its hegemony. Rio de Janeiro reproduced, echoed and projected the dynamics of the Brazilian State: 'The Republic made Rio the mirror of the nation; it is the nation's future made present' (Lessa, 2000:13).

If the dependence on the flow of global financial capital was already high since the 20th century, Brazil has experienced in the last decades a process of accelerated deindustrialisation and *re-primarisation*, that is, an exponential growth of the relative participation of commodities production and export in its economy. This is a consequence of both the increasing demand for commodities on the international market in the first decade of the 2000s and the 'influence' of the political forces connected to the agricultural businesses in recent government coalitions (Lavinas and Gonçalves, 2018). In Rio de Janeiro that meant the establishment of a 'hollow structure of production' that resulted in the profound dismantling of its secondary economic sector (Sobral, 2017: 10–11). Having a small manufacturing sector, the State's taxable revenue remained completely at the mercy of oil and gas revenues (Sobral, 2018: 9). That's why, when the commodities' prices on the international market began to fall starting in 2009, the public deficit's increase became inevitable.

Rio de Janeiro suffered much more intensely than the other regions of the country the impacts from any global or national crisis. Accordingly, Rio de Janeiro has experienced, in recent years, record amounts of unemployment as well as frequent cases of suspension of public service provisions, public employees' salaries and deep cuts in social spending and public investments. The State accepted a Fiscal Recovery Regime as a condition for a bailout plan financed by the Federal Government and based on loans that required radical measures of austerity, comparable, in some ways, with the outcome of the Greek debt crisis from 2010 (Noronha, 2017).

At the same time, the State of Rio de Janeiro has considerably increased the repressive state apparatus and the political violence on different levels – from the criminalisation of protests against austerity policies to the assassination of Marielle Franco, a leftist councilwoman; from the federal intervention of public security to the sentence that convicted 23 activists who were demonstrating during the country-wide protests in June 2013, with a sanction of up to 7 years of imprisonment (Gonçalves and Machado, 2018).

This conservative wave was accompanied by the expansion of paramilitary organisations (militias) and their direct activities in public and institutional spaces. Additionally, as if erasing the border between lawful and unlawful, Rio also turned into the epicentre of corruption scandals. And, finally, in 2016, the city of Rio de Janeiro elected as mayor a neo-Pentecostal bishop with clear far-right tendencies. In the 2018 general elections a conservative and authoritarian judge, Wilson Witzel, who openly defends the extrajudicial 'slaughter' of suspected criminals was elected governor, notwithstanding the election of the far-right President Jair Bolsonaro, who received no less than 70.8 % of the total votes in the state of Rio de Janeiro. Between economic and fiscal crises, State violence and corruption, there is no way to avoid Carvalho's 2019 conclusion that once again, we are consigned to the previously cited Lessa: 'Rio is Brazil, and the future of Brazil is compromised!' (Carvalho, 2019).

Expropriation, violence, and authoritarianism

As shown, the global, national crises and the crises in Rio de Janeiro and in the port region of Rio de Janeiro are intertwined. They required an aggressive cycle of expropriations in terms of rights, contracts, public and common goods and services. The logic has been to explore the potential of the (re)commodification of spaces that are already not-commodified or that have been decommodified and that have the chance to bring relief to situations of capital overaccumulation (of the overproduction of bonds, the overvalorisation of financial actives, real estate bubbles, etc.) (Harvey, 2010).

Such expropriations have been symbolically as well as physically violent. As acts of explicit employment of coercion and force, they are methods that do not

78 *Crisis anchored at the port*

depend on the approval of those being expropriated and, in fact, increase social conflicts. As processes of cutting social rights, dispossession of common land and the privatisation of social goods and collective services, these expropriations confront popular demands (Gonçalves and Machado, 2018: 22). As a consequence of increasing frustrations, social disapproval and protests, the current aggressive cycle of expropriation has generated disturbances in the institutional structures and rules and regulations of the contemporary political systems.

Pressured by the violent character of the expropriations, these systems have produced authoritarian legislation and amplified the repressive instruments of the State. On the one hand, to relieve the anti-popular character of the expropriations, such systems have consented to the ascension of discourses and actors that combine punitive actions, blaming the 'other' and constructing fictitious enemies (Gonçalves and Machado, 2018: 22–23). Seen through this lens, the nexus between the contemporary overaccumulation crisis and the rise of the far-right in diverse parts of the world becomes obvious. Such a rise enables the reframing of social tensions within a chauvinistic matrix, which artificially creates groups supposedly guilty for the current state of affairs, and with that, enemies to fight against: the foreigner, the gay, the woman or the communist (Lavinas and Gonçalves, 2018). Consequently, claims for more repression increase. Thus, the current aggressive cycle of expropriation develops in a vicious circle in which the manner of relief from the socially disruptive effect of the expropriations, in turn, strengthens the repressive State apparatus, and with that, authorises the intensifications of violent methods of expropriation. The attempts to protect expropriating governments contribute to increasing their expropriation power even further. Hence, the diffusion of the crises has led to the expansion of authoritarian rules.

This type of domination clearly challenges the normative foundations of the previous hegemonic pattern of mediation between capitalism and democracy, according to which the extension of democratic rights legitimated capitalist expansion. Following this pattern, a legitimation crisis appears, if political systems are no longer able to articulate mass loyalty (Habermas, 1973; Offe, 1983). Essentially, this prognosis of capitalism's legitimacy problems has not been confirmed: in the context of the radicalisation of the financial and neoliberal accumulation, new motivational resources and means of regulation (Boltanski and Chiapello, 2005) as well as instruments of the rule of law have been mobilised to sustain the expansion of speculative financial capitalism (Picciotto, 2011). Also not empirically confirmed is the expected erosion of State power in the context of the loss of legitimacy of contemporary political systems. On the contrary: the claim for more State control has increased. This demand requires another type of authority that privileges practical strategies of achieving obedience, whether it is through methods of coercion, or through mobilisation of diffused fears.

In the current cycle of expropriation emerges a model of authority that is near the findings of Araujo (2016) in her innovative research on the relations of domination in Chilean society. According to the author, in that case there is no search for consensual or reconciled obedience, but rather, fear of subordinates. Accordingly, authoritarianism is a sort of preventive behaviour motivated by the chronic fear of subordinates, which ruling classes have (Araujo, 2016: 24). Such fear is also felt in contemporary expropriations, above all in the aspirations for order and security that the crises have provoked. Such aspirations do not ask for legitimacy, but rather for the concrete exercise of an effective and efficient authority. In these contexts, as Araujo (2016: 34) demonstrates, the fear of the subordinates is the permanent shadow of failure, with the counterpart requiring strong and discretionary commands. Such fear, above all in conditions of crises, passes through society and reorders multiple social hierarchies (within the family, at school, at work, in politics, etc.). This permits the fear to be socially generalised and experienced by everyone in the double reality of authority, in the command and in the obedience: *ego,* as *alter,* experiments or rejects the authority (for example, in the judgments about how the political authorises acts) that they themselves want to impose (Araujo, 2016: 23–25). There is, with that, the diffusion of the exercising of an authoritarian rule.

The fear of the subordinates ruling classes have also covers the authority of the expropriation practices, and, consequently, its own success. This fear, as seen, is a generalised fear that, if there were no authoritarianism, it would be impossible to exercise command (Araujo, 2016: 83). So, although pillage, dispossession, robberies or frauds generate disillusion and dissent, they are filled with an authoritarian canon, according to which only a 'hard' form of exercising power can be efficient, especially in times of crisis.

In contexts of crises, while such expropriations increase insecurity and precariousness, the authoritarian exercising of power becomes even more widespread. It performs a double function: integrative and repressive. The former refers to the use of rhetorical blaming techniques on the 'other', generating cleavages amongst those impacted by crises, but also, paradoxically, creating a minimum social consensus in repositioning the fear onto the subordinates (who turn into the 'other'). At the same time, it defends the reinforcement of the repressive state apparatus as a solution against the 'other' who can question authority. The crisis turns therefore into a combustible for a regime of expropriators who engage in an intense exercise of authority.

In the next paragraphs, we will examine in close detail each one of these crises, their chains and interconnections, as well as the expropriations, State violence and authoritarian regimes that accompany them.

Global crisis

As we saw in Chapter 1, the first decade of the 21st century encountered an overproduction of fictitious assets based on the indebtedness of North American families, above all through the mortgage loans given by the banks in the form of a risky credit without guarantees (subprimes). This overproduction manifested itself in the creation of a financial bubble based on securitisation practices. That is: to avoid the illiquidity of mortgage returns in the long run, the banks left them out of their balances, transforming this mass of credits into different bonds and tradable derivatives. Well supported by credit rating agencies, these bonds were

80 *Crisis anchored at the port*

easily sold for a value much higher than the original debts. Since the banks could easily recover the worth of the loans as mortgages, they could also restart the same operation with the emission of new fictitious assets (Altvater, 2010).

That is how a bubble was growing, that, however, provided a real guarantee: the growth of the housing prices and the consequential real estate wealth that could mobilise new loans (Saad Filho, 2011: 247). According to Kotz (2009: 311),

> By the summer of 2007 housing prices had risen by 70% corrected for infla-
> tion since 1995. At its peak in 2007, the housing bubble created an estimated
> $8 trillion in inflated new housing wealth, out of total housing wealth of
> $20 trillion, or 40% of housing wealth.

As the price and the real estate wealth depend on the increase of family consumption, the high housing prices started gradually being unsustainable in the context of the long neoliberal era of salary stagnation and fiscal adjustments, accompanied by the increase of tax on interest (Saad Filho, 2011: 247–248). When the wave of defaults began, the dispersion of the crisis became inevitable. The bubble burst. It started what is considered to be the second-worst financial crisis in the history of capitalism.

Reconstructing each step of each respective crisis (which unfolded in the collapse of financial institutions, with repercussions in the 'real economy' such as the bankruptcy of *General Motors* etc.) goes beyond the scope of this work. However, it is important to state that the answer adopted by the governments and economic powers has been based on the rule of 'saving the financial system and the redistribution of the burden on the public' (Gonçalves and Machado, 2018: 22). The United States government, for example, transferred between December 2007 and June 2010 $16 trillion through the Federal Reserve to private banks and investment agencies with interest rates close to zero (Sanders, 2011). This reorientation of the public debts now canalised for protecting the financial system became even more clear in 2010, when the European Union, under the leadership of Germany, imposed a reduction of public deficits as an anti-crisis measure for Greece (Gonçalves and Machado, 2018: 22).

The equation formulated accurately by Altvater (2010: 10), 'the debt burden for many = benefits for the inflow of incomes and interest of credits for the few' has accelerated and dramatically increased the scale of the expropriation process on a global level. Such expropriations manifested themselves in diverse ways. The most immediate and evident is the expropriation of the established rights of workers even in countries with consolidated welfare regimes. Just think about as an example how, as Dörre and Holst (2010: 37) demonstrate, in Germany 'from the 64% of the population that belongs to the middle class, close to 20% now live under *precarious prosperity*' and that 'one-fifth of the job force has already lost their job one or two times, with the tendency continuing to rise'.

However, the most evident example for the expropriation prescription that has been applied since the 2008 crisis is the Greek case. In 2015, the creditors negotiating the Greek debt, represented by the so-called *Troika*, which was, the Central European Bank, the International Monetary Fund and the European Commission, imposed

Crisis anchored at the port 81

unilaterally a strict regime of austerity in return for rescue programs and financial help. In order to produce primary budget surplus, Greece was forced, among other measures, to adopt of an automatic system of expenditures cuts (without approval from the parliament), to increase of the value added tax (VAT), which is concerned with consumption (for example, of medicine, basic food products, water and electricity), to implement a radical program of privatisation (whose assets were transferred to a fund whose interests would pay new loans and recapitalise banks), to broadly reform the pension system (applying, even, a zero deficit clause) and revising labour legislation, including the legal provision for collective dismissals (Nunes, 2015). The Greek example represents a culmination in the extremely aggressive cycle of direct expropriations of rights, contracts, goods and public and collective services.

This cycle of expropriations is also characterised by a dizzying rhythm of primary expropriations of land and of natural resources that primarily affected the Global South. Since 2008, the global demand for land has exponentially grown (Sauer and Leite, 2012: 873). Since a large part of this land is in Latin America, and above all, in Africa, scholars refer to this cycle of land grabbing as a true 'tropical banquet' (Boechat, Pitta & Toledo, 2017: 76).

This cycle has been confronted with protests of those affected by the crisis and worsened by the adopted solution. Think about, for example, in movements like *Occupy Wall Street* and its slogan *'we are the 99 percent'* that then expanded to social fights in many other countries and openly criticised the excessive concentration of wealth and power of the richest 1% in the world. Such movements take place in a global context of pervasive indignation against the political and financial system that hatched after the global financial crisis of 2008 (Bringel & Pleyers, 2017). Within these, the protests in 2011 in southern Europe became particularly well known, above all in Spain, as well as the fights for the free-tuition university in Chile. A new wave of indignation hatched in the following years in other locations such as in the Arab world (the Arab Spring), in Turkey (Gezi Park) and in Brazil (the June Journeys of 2013).

Such protests indicate not only that the expropriations unleashed ample social disapproval, but also the need to develop forms of 'protest immunisation' in order to guarantee the effectiveness of these expropriations. In this context, State violence and the implementation of authoritarian instruments grow. They serve to 'neutralise' popular demands contrary to the policies of adjustment and austerity and to force the acceptance of measures that are profoundly anti-social. The most extreme example of this is once again the Greek case. Against the state of outrage produced by the multiple expropriative laws, the Greek people erupted in 2015 into movements and protests that ended in a referendum in which a clear majority (61.3%) rejected the bail-out project of the international creditors. This emphatic rejection did not help: under the liquidity crisis of the Greek banks and the fear of the threats and economic consequences from Greece leaving the Euro zone, the leftist party Syriza, which was elected to reverse the social cuts, accepted the agreement with the *Troika* described above.

All of these authoritarian measures, which ignore popular sovereignty, have been reinterpreted by Streeck (2016:47–50) as a continuous process and gradual degradation of the relations of capitalism and democracy. In this sense, the global

82 Crisis anchored at the port

crisis would be undermining all of the mediation mechanisms, among them social Keynesian policy, the principles of political representation and legal liberalism, that, consolidated in the post-war, have appeased the conflicts between capitalism and democracy. Starting from the distinction between 'egalitarian democracy' and 'market-confirming democracy', the author argues that the latter would be in complete conformity with the Hayekianismo neoliberal, creating hyper commodification of the political decisions (Streeck, 2015:105–106).

Although Streeck's approach presents a certain idealistic, Eurocentric and gender bias that distorts his perception of the material conditions of democracy (also of the post-war), it reveals the extension of authoritarianism that the current aggressive cycle of expropriations implies. Such authoritarianism has continuously strengthened actors, parties and movements of the far-right. As demonstrated, the crisis has reinforced inequalities, privatisation and pressured more and more contingents to seek to satisfy their necessities on the market. At the same time, the middle and working classes are seeing the reduction of their status and their political and economic power. The far-right reframes this social lowering through the xenophobic and chauvinistic lenses to construct barriers against immigrants and refugees. For strengthening authoritarian models of authority, the fear of the other has allowed the growth of far-right social movements, such as, for example, Pegida in Germany, and the electoral success of politicians with fascist tendencies. This is the case for, among others, Donald Trump, Viktor Orbán, Andrzej Duda and Jair Bolsonaro.

The Brazilian crisis

Unfortunately, the prophecy of the former president Luiz Inácio Lula da Silva, according to which Brazil would not be affected by the global financial crisis of 2008, did not become a reality. The crisis in form of 'tsunami in the United States' did not only reach Brazil, but, when it arrived, it submerged the country's economy in a flood that still persists[1]. The crisis profoundly affected the main socioeconomic bases of the country and it has continuously reached new heights, each time more critical, unfolding political, social, institutional and cultural tensions. We are confronted with multiple crises that are spatially synchronised connecting different focal points, causes and effects. Deindustrialisation, abrupt falls of commodities prices, mass protests, fiscal deficits, high debt in the population, partisanship in the judicial system, the collapse of the political system, and dismantling of social programs and a far-right electoral victory are manifestations of a growing state of disarticulation of the bases on which just a short while before was seated a democratic coexistence in a society marked by abysmal inequalities.

Between 2003 and 2014, the system of power defined by A. Singer (2012) as *lulismo*, referencing a period in which Brazil was governed by Lula da Silva (2003–2009) and by his hand-picked successor, Dilma Rousseff (2010–2016), demonstrated to be extremely successful, electorally as well as in the promotion of economic growth. From a social point of view, lulismo represented an alliance of classes, which on one side promoted orthodox economic policies, combining

Crisis anchored at the port 83

high interest rates, fluctuating exchange rates and a balanced public budget, and on the other side permitted a significant increase of social spending and the raising of the minimum wage. In the period between 2003 and 2014, the real minimum wage grew 75%, the percentage of poor people in Brazilian society reduced by half and the Gini index referring to income reduced from 0.59 to 0.51. However, since 2015, it has already grown once again, reaching 0.54 in 2017 (CEPAL, 2019: 37). At the same time, the wealthiest Brazilians particularly benefited from the GDP growing 64% during that same period. The tax system funded on the taxation of the salaries and the consumption and the waiver of taxing capital gains permitted the Brazilian millionaires to improve their social position under *lulism*. Today, 10% of the wealthiest in Brazil have seized 38% of the total income – the largest concentration of all the Latin American countries. For comparisons sake, 10% of the wealthiest in Argentina have 21% of the income (CEPAL, 2019: 39). In respect to properties and other assets, the concentration was even larger. Four hundred thousand income tax payers who are around 0.2% of the Brazilian population, in 2012 concentrated 48% of all of the declared wealth in the country (Castro, 2014).

From a parliamentary political point of view, lulismo maintained and amplified the rationale of formation of parliamentary majorities traditionally prevalent in Brazilian politics, which means, the distribution of the spaces of power in the State (job posts, control of State businesses, control of the budget of public agencies and ministries, etc.) so that the government supporters could establish legal or illegal negotiations with their allies and economic agents to the benefit of their parties or their own pockets. So, for example, the party that controlled the Ministry of Transportation guaranteed that its deputies and senators supported the projects presented by the executive. At the same time, the Ministry negotiated overpriced contracts with the companies that constructed roads and highways or controlled privatised highways so that part of the profit extorted from the State could return to the party's treasuries or to the private accounts of individual politicians. Another often used procedure, particularly with large exporter of meats, was to issue through the State Bank of Development (BNDES) loans with favourable conditions so that part of the loan would return to the party's treasury or to the politicians' pockets.

Lulismo worked during the cycle of rapid economic growth, when all of the sectors in society saw their material conditional improve. The GDP plummeted, however, from 7.6% in 2010 to 0.1% in 2014, contracting to 3.5% in 2015 and 3.6% in 2016. In 2017 and 2018, the GDP grew again, but just at 1.1% per year, much less than the projections (O Globo, 2017a). Starting in 2015, the corruption investigations hardened, obstructing the access channels to public money and to the conveniences offered by the State to the large firms, particularly from the finance sector, agricultural business and public construction works. In this moment, the alliance of classes constructed by lulismo broke and the accumulated tensions manifested in the streets through mass demonstrations as well as in the parliamentary arena, culminating with the impeachment of President Dilma Rousseff in 2016 under the very fragile argument that she had manipulated public

84 *Crisis anchored at the port*

accounts. The impeachment of the president and her replacement by the vice-president Temer, who was also denounced for corruption, gave embodiment to the effort to revert the power and material losses suffered during the crisis by some groups. Accordingly, the aggressive policy of the privatisation and the advantages offered to the agribusiness companies and the extensive cuts of workers' rights adopted during Temer's government (2016–2018), among other measures, clearly indicate not only the effort to reopen the access channels to State resources to the most rich, but also the commitment to reconfigure the distributive arrangement in favour of capital and against the workers (Costa and Motta 2019). Similarly, the closing by Temer of agencies and the suspension of policies dedicated to the promotion of gender and racial equality can be interpreted as a reaction to the little reduction of the material and power asymmetries between men and women and blacks and whites, promoted by lulismo.[2]

The tenor of Bolsonaro's presidential campaign in 2018 as well as the first measures adopted by him as the new Brazilian President starting in January 2019 strengthen the expectation that his government will develop the venture that Temer began, but, due to the absolute lack of legitimacy and by the weight of the corruption allegations against him, was not possible for Temer to complete. This implies reverting of the few benefits obtained by the poor and minorities in the period of lulismo and to once again guarantee full access to the State's resources for the rich.

Indeed, the disqualification by Bolsonaro of policies of promotion of racial and gender equality as victimisation ('coitadismo'), the pride in that he declared having voted against legislation that gave domestic workers similar rights to those enjoyed by the rest of the workers and the decision, as President, to adjust the minimum wage to under the maximum rate denoted by the law represent unequivocal demonstrations of his disinterest for the poor and minorities. Additionally, the announced tax reform to reduce the maximum rate of income tax of the highest income brackets from 27.5% to 20% (PSL, 2018), as well as the attempts to reduce restrictions imposed by environmental laws on the expansion of economic activities and his efforts to making the borders of agro-business advance over indigenous reservations or protected areas are clear indications that the Bolsonaro administration wants to expand the power and economic spaces of the richest Brazilians in detriment of the poor, the minorities and the environmental preservation.

The very ministerial cabinet built by Bolsonaro confirmed this double objective, meaning, to undo the small advances in the fight against inequality and asymmetries of power observed during lulismo and to create new advantages for the most privileged sectors. Accordingly, while the ministries of economy, agriculture, infrastructure and regional development are occupied by people with some expertise and experience in mainstream economies, the ministry of education, the ministry of women, family, and human rights, together with the ministry of foreign affairs are occupied by bizarre figures and who are without adequate professional qualifications. Their function seems to be rather ideologically fighting against leftist and progressive forces than to properly develop a sound ministerial work program; for this they lack basic skills.

Until the moment that this book was finished in May 2019, it did not seem apparent that the government based on this schizophrenic composition could retrieve the country from its deep political, economic, social and institutional crises. On the contrary, Bolsonaro's alleged intention of governing without bargaining advantages in the government for his parliamentary basis clearly shows its unfeasibility. In the same way, the process of the partisan judicial, with its decision of investigation and punishment clearly founded not in the impartiality of the law but on the political preferences of the justice system's operators, does not give any sign of being reversed.

The Rio de Janeiro crisis

When handling the Rio de Janeiro crisis, the press has frequently played metaphors that allude to a trajectory from glory to mud, from euphoria to depression or from honeymoon to collapse (*El Pais*, 2016a; 2017). Whereas these images fulfil a function of representing reactions to the frustration of the expectations in contexts of crisis, they say, however, little about the condition, the character, or the dynamic and effects of the actual crisis.

From the beginning, it is necessary to ask about the phase of success. If, throughout the 20th century, the Rio economy gradually lost its productive dynamism (and this is for diverse reasons, such as the end of the priority of its economy with the rise of the industrial São Paulo and the national centering with the move of the capital to Brasília), the Brazilian deindustrialisation, launched in the last decades, consolidated the scene of deterioration (Sobral, 2017; 2018). While, in this period, the participation of Rio de Janeiro in Brazil's manufactural sector (where there are qualified job opportunities, higher incomes and formal employment) was drastically reduced, the size of its oil sector was higher than in the rest of Brazil (O Globo, 2015).

Rio followed, thus, the tendency of the national economy of expanding its extractive sector, pulled by the so-called commodity boom at the start of the 21st century (2000–2014) that brought significant rises in prices of primary products (food, metals, petroleum, etc.). Paradoxically, that did not lead to the rise of the weight of Rio's participation in the Brazilian GDP. As Sobral (2018: 7) demonstrates, the State of Rio de Janeiro, between 1995 and 2013, has maintained a low participation of 11%, in the national added value, that is the total value created by Brazilian economy.

Due to its extremely fragile and dependent economic basis, the impact of the collapse of commodity prices in the State Rio de Janeiro was especially devastating. Accordingly, the same process that happened on the national level and that, as demonstrated, impoverished the country and spiralled it into a deep economic recession, was not only felt in the most intense form, but was found in its epicentre, Rio de Janeiro. The period that followed the state of emergency declared in 2016, just some weeks before the Olympic games started, was marked by the suspension of public works and investments, the diminishment and even suspension of funds transferred to universities, schools, hospitals, housing projects and

86 *Crisis anchored at the port*

urban reforms, the interruption of policies and of essential services. The payment of salaries of public servants from various State sectors (education, health, science, and technology, insurance, etc.) was, first, paid in instalments and then later, completely suspended. It was a state of devastation with the cancellation of activities in essential sectors, such as, for example, teaching institutions and health centres (*El Pais*, 2017). The State government applied, in this manner, an aggressive policy of expropriation based on indiscriminate measures of fiscal austerity that plundered rights, collective goods, and above all, the means of subsistence for active, inactive and retired public employees.[3]

Despite the consensus regarding the impact of the commodity crisis on the public accounts in Rio, the discussions on possible solutions treated it as a conjunctural and not as a structural problem failing to measure the real dimension of the persistence of the fiscal deficit. Additionally, using the justification of supporting the conduction of the Football World Cup (2014) and the Olympic Games in the city of Rio de Janeiro, Rio's government adopted a wide-ranging policy of tax waiving, liberating various transactions of paying the local valued added tax ICMS. Cislaghi et al. (2016: 7) demonstrate that, between 2008 and 2012, R\$ 138.6 billion were conceded in tax exemptions. Such exemptions benefited petroleum firms, gas and the automotive sector, public transportation companies and electric energy and even sectors of luxury consumption, such as beauty and jewellery services (Cislaghi et al., 2016: 7). Among the sponsors of the Olympics, companies like Coca-Cola, McDonald's and the Brazilian media giant Globo were benefitted as well.

Nonetheless, the government discourse, at both the State and Federal levels, tried to link the fiscal shortages to the budget being compromised at the expense of the personnel, and above all, to account for the deficits in the pensions system. However, regarded comparatively in proportion to the GDP, household income and public income liquid accounts, the active personnel expenditures of the Rio government is one of the lowest, if not the lowest, in Brazil (Sobral, 2018: 19). Furthermore, Rio de Janeiro's government adopts generalised practices of outsourcing and commissioned functions, reducing, according to Sobral, the financing sources of the pensions' system (Sobral, 2018: 20).

Besides the fiscal problems, Rio de Janeiro government's discourses were not able to sufficiently mobilise popular acceptance and to construct a minimum level of legitimacy for the expropriation measures of austerity that have been adopted. The lack of legitimacy was aggravated by the corruption scandals involving recent governors and others leading the final management decisions that were taken by the State government. The ex-governor Sergio Cabral Filho (2006–2014) was put in prison in November 2016. He was responsible for active and passive corruption, money laundering, tax evasion, organised crime, cartel formation and bid rigging. He was already convicted nine times and condemned for almost 200 years of prison. The former governor Luiz Fernando Pezão (2014–2018), for his turn, was also in prison in November 2018. He was accused of receiving more than R\$ 29 million through corruption schemes and for integrating the political core of a criminal organisation that committed a variety of crimes against the

Crisis anchored at the port   87

public administration. Finally, Francisco Dornelles, vice-governor (2015–2018) and acting governor in different periods, was accused together with Pezão for corruption involving exactly the fiscal exemptions: both had given facilities encompassing more than R$ 2 billion to firms that donated illegal money to an electoral campaign in 2014 (G1 2018a; 2018b; 2018c).

It is certain that the euphoria surrounding the 'Olympic City' and the expectations that the Olympic mega event would bring development would not come to fruition. On the contrary, the option for high investments directed at entertainment, including arenas and sport parks, boulevards, golf places, etc., illuminated the typical contradictions of the modernisation projects, in that what 'is called "modern" grows and nourishes from the existence of the "backward"' (Oliveira, 1972: 7–8) or, to use our terminology, in which expropriations and, for that matter, the deepening inequality, are conditions for the transformation of physical space into economic value.

Four main projects are icons of these contrasts: the luxurious Olympic Park constructed after a violent removal next to the 20 remaining homes of the poor district 'Vila Autódromo'; the renovation of the Maracanã Stadium, a neighbour of the Rio de Janeiro State University that, without resources, did not work; the so-called transolympic *Bus Rapid Transit (*BRT) whose walls divide the pompous Athletes Villages and the remnant families of the Vila União de Curicica favela, who live without basic sanitary services, at the mercy of the open sewage and, finally, the Porto Maravilha and the favelas in the port region, of which we will discuss in more detail below. During the Olympic Games, a general feeling of unrest prevailed as expressed by one of the main leaders of the anti-austerity fight, Lia Rocha: 'We gave our house [for the celebrations] but we were not invited for the party' (BBC Brasil, 2016b).

This scene of social precariousness and violence explained the large support of the population for the shutdowns, protests and demonstrations, above all among public servants, including teachers, health professionals, firefighters, police officers, penitentiary officers, etc. In April 2016, workers for the State of Rio from 33 categories began to strike. The transit department stopped completely. In November of the same year, a group of protesters, mostly police officers, invaded the Legislative Assembly of the State of Rio de Janeiro. A significant part of these movements was motivated according to DIEESE (2017: 28) by an immediate and urgent reason: the delayed payment of the salaries. On the other hand, these and similar movements also fought for protecting State institutions and the provision of public goods and services, as became evident in the school occupations by high school students and in the fights conducted by public servants for continuing governmental transfers for the maintenance of public services (G1, 2016).

From the perspective of the capitalist expropriations, social movements opposed to the compression of public space and services which do not operate with the strict logic of the market. This cycle of protests, as seen, is anchored in a widespread social disapproval in relation to the government of Rio de Janeiro and its policies. These movements reached partial but important success both in relation to the discharge of delayed salaries, the regular payment and the reissuing

88 *Crisis anchored at the port*

of the government transfers and also in terms of protection of public institutions from the constant threats and proposals of privatisation, the elimination of the gratuity of public services, mass lay-offs, etc.

On the other side, ignoring the popular rejection and social protests, negotiations between the Federal and State governments brought more austerity policies, like, for example, the law that raised the contribution rate to the pensions of the service workers from 11–14% (G1, 2017a). As seen, such negotiations culminated in a plan to recover Rio's public debt in September 2017, the Fiscal Recovery Regime. This Regime introduced a fiscal adjustment plan, similar to a solution *à la Greek* imposed in the context of the global and national crisis.

Insensitive to the popular demands and to the necessity of the approval from those affected by the measures it implies, the fiscal recuperation regime operated in circumstances of elevated social dissent and the acceleration of expropriations of rights and subsistence means. Accordingly, its implementation was accompanied by an increase of violence and of the repressive State apparatus by political means of social control, criminalisation of protests and of poverty. The demonstrations and strikes of public servants were met by the truculent actions of the military police who widely used tear gas bombs, weapons with rubber bullets and anti-riot gear to disperse protesters.

To assure discussions and voting on the austerity measures, the Legislative Assembly of the State of Rio remained roped-off by an isolation cord, formed by armed vehicles, rails and cavalry. It became frequent that the protests during that time ended with repression and injured protesters. When the voting of the first wave of austerity occurred, the police action was truculent, with tear gas reaching even the voting chamber in the Parliament and ironically, the deputies approved the bill using gas masks (O Globo, 2017).

The State violence was joined by *pari passu* the increase of austerity policies. Synchronised to the repressive policies adopted by former President Temer, the State of Rio triggered the same decree of the *Guarantee of Law and Order* that the Federal Government used against protests in the Federal Capital. So, in the same manner of how there was an expansion of military presence in the core government in Brasília, Rio also became militarised (Gonçalves and Machado, 2018: 23).

Beyond the 2018 carnival, federal intervention was announced for the public security of the State of Rio de Janeiro, which lasted until the 31st of December of the same year, under the responsibility of a military leader, General Braga Netto. With this, the police's power passed on to be under the control of the Armed Forces. According to the report by the Intervention Observatory (CESEC, 2019), the intervention caused a clear increase in the use of lethal force by the police. The number of massacres (54 during the intervention, bringing a total of 216 dead people) grew 63.6%, when compared to the same period in 2017. From the more than 6,000 violent deaths in all of the State during that period, 22.7% were committed by police and military. According to the coordinator of the Observatory, Silvia Ramos, this cycle of violence was generated by an 'omission in the Armed Forces' command in relation to police brutality' (UOL, 2019). Omissions like this explain the massacre in the Fallet-Foqueteiro slum, on the 12th of January 2019, which ended in 15 deaths – the worst massacre in Rio de Janeiro since 2007 (UOL, 2019).

The federal intervention consolidated attack against rights, liberties and guarantees in the favelas of Rio. It added to the dominant punitive discourse the allusion of values such as discipline, honesty and fighting the enemy. This has worked as a stigmatisation mechanism of a social group characterised as deviant, that, in the case of the federal intervention in Rio, are the favelas' inhabitants. As deviants they do not need to be protected. Synonymous with criminality and drug trafficking, reconfigured as enemies, those living in the favela can be, in any moment and without observing any constitutional guarantees, dispossessed, violated, raped, robbed and assassinated. The increase in the level of authoritarianism of the State and the use of stigmatizing discourses have increasingly created a space for fascist discourses that preached the elimination of the 'other' (Gonçalves and Machado, 2018).

During the federal intervention, the black councilwoman, born and raised in the Favela Maré, from the Socialist and Liberty Party (PSOL), Marielle Franco, and her driver, Anderson Gomes, were assassinated on March 14th, 2018, a crime with a clear political motivation. Critical of the abuses of the police raids in the favelas, she was the rapporteur of the Commission of the City Council of Rio, created to accompany the intervention. Only one year after the assassination, in March 2019, the police were able to identify and arrest the presumed perpetrators, two contract killers associated with Rio de Janeiro's militias. The assassinations have reaffirmed the fluidness of the borders separating criminal organisations and the State apparatus; there legality and illegality, State order and paramilitary, lawless violence are rather complementary than antagonistic forces sustaining expropriations. Furthermore, the current senator, Flavio Bolsonaro, a fascist-oriented activist and son of the Republic's president, has been investigated due to his connections with the mercenaries involved in crimes including the assassinations of Marielle Franco and her driver (*El Pais*, 2019). Once again, Rio de Janeiro is a Brazil *en miniature*, 'and the future of Brazil is compromised'!

In summary, the fiscal recuperation regime as an answer to the crisis in Rio de Janeiro refers to a triple development. In the first place, it creates conditions that commodify spaces that were not yet fully commodified through expropriative acts. This can be verified in how part of the Rio population is pushed towards the market as social rights are cancelled and public services privatised. Dependents on private provision (for health, education, pensions, etc.) – these groups need to draw on banking debts to take care of their basic necessities (Lavinas and Gonçalves, 2018). In the second place, without any plan of industrial restructuration or political anti-cyclical fighting against the economic recession, the fiscal recuperation regime has only served to stabilise the public debt (Sobral, 2018: 21). Once stable, government bonds are used by finance capital for participating in processes of privatisation and securitisation. The first and the second developments converge insofar as both enable the expropriation of means of subsistence of different social groups and the transfer of State resources to private investors

90 *Crisis anchored at the port*

who benefit from interest payments of the public debt and other instruments of public fund privatisation (Cislaghi, 2017: 151).

In the third place, in front of the risks of social disappointment and dissent, the State violence and, above all, the federal intervention emerges as the populist response to the anxiety for security, and, at the same time, as an effort to create a minimum social consensus. Paradoxically, the intervention with its repressive machine enables Rio de Janeiro's government to implement austerity measures that are socially disruptive (Gonçalves and Machado 2018). In mobilizing pervasive feelings and fears in the population, the federal intervention represents the repressive state apparatus as a necessary practice in a moment of crisis. It works in parallel, as seen, as a way of stigmatisation and blaming of the 'other' (the 'thugs', the favela inhabitants) for the social maladies. There has been, then, a construction of a type of authority that is not found based in persuasion, but in the strengthening of the very repressive apparatus. This type of authority presented during the intervention as the only salvation for Rio de Janeiro 'enabled the loan agreement between the federal government and the government of the State of Rio de Janeiro, crucial for overcoming the financial crisis in which Rio has found itself since 2016' (Ramos, 2019: 32). The intervention served to consolidate a pattern of accumulation based on unlimited expropriations. That is, the intervention worked as a protection shield that allows expropriations by the subjection of the expropriated and the protection against social protests. In this context, social dissatisfaction is neutralised by giving responsibility for all problems to the constructed other, the favela inhabitant, the criminals, the leftists, etc. This combination has driven a strengthening and gradual acceptance of authoritarian authority.

The State violence and the authoritarian authority have been key factors to guarantee the expansion of capital accumulation in Rio de Janeiro. They eliminate the resistances against a bail-out arrangement based on expropriation practices, that through different forms of privatisation and recommodification (re)connect large investors, governmental agencies, private concessionaires, real estate corporations, construction companies, politicians and also criminal organisations (militias, corruption nets, etc.). These pressures for (re)articulating accumulation are especially visible when the crisis landed in the port region of Rio de Janeiro.

Crisis at the port

Finance capital, the real estate market, commercial ventures, businesses, government actors and the mainstream media euphorically accompanied the start of the Project Porto Maravilha. The magnitude of investments in the urban reform – 'the largest public–private partnership of Brazil'— fed the optimistic economic expectations and the positive scenarios designed at that time. As we saw in the previous chapter, the square meter price throughout the whole region grew intensively in the first months of the project, all of the CEPACs were bought at once at a single auction by the State bank CEF and its unitary price grew in a very rapid manner. The euphoria, however, did not last long. The impact of the Brazilian economic recession and the crisis in Rio were devastating in the port region.

It is true that, even before the respective crises, signals of distrust already existed with the project. The local newspaper specialised in reporting on the economy, Relatório Reservado (2012), already questioned in October 2012 if the CEF had done a good deal, since until then they had not received a single cent from the FIIPM. On the other side, the high prices of petroleum boosted the real estate market in Rio de Janeiro, above all in 2011 (*Jornal do Brasil*, 2017a). Property prices in many different neighbourhoods soared. Various enterprises and companies began to manifest interest in the port region, which, in turn, reinforced the financial expectations of returns for the investment opportunities created by the Project Porto Maravilha. In 2012, various firms announced investments in the area. According to the press at the time, the telecommunication companies Oi and GVT as well as the Central Bank of Brazil intended to move their branches to the region and, for that, they would invest high sums to reform and expand buildings able to accommodate their headquarters (*Brasil Econômico*, 2012). In the same manner, Microsoft announced R$ 200 million for the revitalisation of an historic building that would house a startups' accelerator, an advanced technology laboratory and a development centre for its search platform (*Brasil Econômico*, 2012). Also the construction companies CHL and Sandia announced huge investments in the construction of commercial buildings in the area (Almeida, 2013). In May 2013, one of the most important real estate companies worldwide, the North American Tishman Speyer, clinched a deal for constructing four high-end commercial towers with an investment of over R$ 1 billion (Relatório Reservado, 2013a). In August of the same year, the at the time (only) businessman Donald Trump announced the purchase of two large plots (Relatório Reservado, 2013b). At the beginning of 2014, the Spanish Salamanca Group also declared interest in the region (Relatório Reservado, 2014a).

Even if the distrust still persisted, as expressed, for example, in the continuous rejection of Petros to invest in real estate buildings or in the fact that Trump had meanwhile abandoned the construction projects in the area, the bet of the financial valorisation of the space continued (Relatório Reservado, 2013c; 2014b). Accordingly, the State bank CEF decided, in January 2014, to join the investors of the real estate sector as a partner in the project of constructing five commercial towers in the area (Relatório Reservado, 2014c). Also the project of constructing the Trump Towers continued in another way: the Bulgarian company MRP International, together with the Salamanca Group and the construction company Even, decided to invest R$ 5 billion in the building of the towers and, for marketing reasons, sublet Trump's name for branding the buildings (Relatório Reservado, 2015a).

Next to the 'heating up' of the real estate market, the CEPACs started becoming overrated (Neto, 2013). Originally bought by the CEF, in 2011 for a unitary price of R$ 545, the CEPACs reached in December of 2013 the unitarian price of R$ 1280, an 'expressive height of 135% in a period of 28 months', as Neto (2013) detected. Even if the sale of the CEPACs was much lower than expected, from 2011 to 2014, the FIIPM was able to keep the flow of transfers to the project, which allowed the construction companies that comprised the Concessionary

92 *Crisis anchored at the port*

Porto Novo responsible for the administration of the area, to complete the expected works (*Jornal do Brasil*, 2017b).

Just as we demonstrated in the previous chapter, according to the logic of the public–private partnership, the concessionaire received regular payments from the municipal company CDURP that, for its turn, received resources form the FIIPM. In the moment of market euphoria, this operation appeared to work well. At that time, the project Porto Maravilha was publicly recognised as characterised by high synergy and dynamism in that the interest of the real estate companies in the port region, the bonds offered on the market, the confidence of the private sector and the State initiatives all converged, permitting the flow of different capitals for the reconstruction project and commodification of the entire area.

It is clear that these expectations of the CEPACs' valorisation and of the real estate market were created, formed and nourished in parallel to violent State interventions that restructured the entire port zone. As demonstrated, this reconstruction depended on an extremely violent removal process that expropriated the means of the very subsistence of old inhabitants of the regions, that is, their lodging. From 2009 to 2016, 675 families were expelled from their communities because of the project Porto Maravilha. From the occupied building named Zumbi dos Palmares, which was located in an abandoned building belonging to the National Social Security Institute, 133 families were removed in 2011. In the same year, 30 families from the urban occupation Flor do Asfalto were met with the same fate. In 2012, the occupation Machado de Assis was also cleared. Also completely removed were the families from the occupied areas Boa Vista (35 families), Carlos Marighela (47 families) and Casarão Azul (70 families). Until November 2015, 140 families have been removed and another 692 found themselves threatened by removal in the Hill of Providência due to the alleged risky situation in the area, as well as the implementation of a touristic cable car and an inclined lift. Finally, the occupied area Quilombo das Guerreiras was completely defunct with the removal of its 70 families. Its land was offered to the project *Trump Towers Rio*, described above (Comitê Popular da Copa and Olímpiadas do Rio de Janeiro, 2015; Ziesche et al., 2014).

Until 2015, the port zone underwent an accelerated process of valorisation of different forms of capitals (finance, real estate, commercial ventures and productive capital), nourished by the violent expropriation of spaces hitherto not yet completely commodified. This process exhausted itself with the collapse of the international petroleum price and the impact of the Brazilian economic recession, when the crisis reached Rio de Janeiro. It reproduced, at the level of local actors and structures associated with the project Porto Maravilha, the same mechanisms of instability imposed by the global financialisation, that is, the hyperproduction of fictitious assets which can no longer be turned over within the given socio-economic time and space.

At the port in Rio, this dynamic presented itself as a crisis of overaccumulation of the CEPACs in a context of real estate market retraction in the region. The crisis, itself, activated in the port region processes of decommodification, marked by threats of and also real decline of profit perspectives leading to the suspension of investments in the area. This has led to rearrangements and renegotiations among different forms of capitals and investors involved in the project in order to generate a new wave of commodification and expropriations in response to the crisis and the profit decline. Let's now take a look at each of these reconfigurations.

Between 2011 and 2016, the nominal prices of CEPACs tripled. Taking into account inflation rates in the period, this represents a real valorisation of about 55%. This overvalorisation in the context of declining real estate business is, by itself, an indication that the bonds are being employed as financial speculation (Fundação Getulio Vargas, 2017: 46). Additionally, in 2015, the CEF gave signs that it would revise investments in its joint construction projects in the area. If, from one side, this position reaffirmed the speculative use of CEPACs, on the other, it positioned the real estate companies that already had made investments on alert. The worsening of prospects has been registered by the economic bulletin Relatório Reservado (2015b) along a series of headlines, which are truly epithets of the crisis: 'Empty Rooms', 'Depression Port', 'Ghost Town', 'Ghost Port', 'Olympic Legacy', and 'Rio de Janeiro Pays Its Price'. The coverages refer to the difficulties faced by the real estate company Thishman Speyer, one of the biggest investors in the port region. The company constructed two large towers in the region, the Aqwa Corporate and the Port Corporate, but it was not able to rent out the majority of the constructed offices even after successive discounts in the rent price (Relatório Reservado, 2016, 2017a, 2017b). In 2018, in both buildings, Aqwa Corporate and Port Corporate, the value of the location that, in 2009, began at R\$ 160/square metre had already been reduced to R\$ 60/square metre. Despite this, various units remained unrented (Relatório Reservado, 2018a).

The case of the company Thishman Speyer is paradigmatic for the shrinkage of the real estate market of Rio de Janeiro and in the port area. In July 2017, the index of the empty commercial properties in Rio de Janeiro was 89% (*Jornal do Brasil*, 2017a; Relatório, 2017c). Since 2017 only very few large firms have continued investing in the port area. As Werneck et al. (2018) shows, only a few construction projects started in the port area have been finished. More and more, the interest has turned from the construction of high towers to 'the reforms of the small commercial spaces [...]' (Werneck et al., 2018: 6–7).

The nonexistence of new constructions corroded the finance mechanism of Porto Maravilha. Thus, the less CEPACs for real estate business' ends are sold, the lesser the amount of resources available to pay the urban reform and maintenance of the port area. This resulted in the State bank CEF recognizing that such bonds were stuck and that the FIIPM, that was under its control, lacked liquidness (Agência Brasil, 2017; *Diário do Porto*, 2018), which evidently does not cancel its obligation to regularly pay the concessionary responsible for the maintenance of the area. To fulfil this obligation, in 2015, the CEF, once again, dipped into the reserves of the workers' pension fund FGTS, that it manages. It used more than R\$ 1.5 billion of workers' savings to salvage the FIIPM (*Diário do Porto*, 2018; *Jornal do Comércio*, 2017).

Obviously, this did not solve the problem. In May 2016, the FIIPM had just R\$ 217.7 million available, but needed to make at least R\$ 1.2 billion accessible for

94 *Crisis anchored at the port*

the sixth stage of construction work in the region (Agência Brasil, 2017; *Jornal do Comércio*, 2017). At this time, the declaration of illiquidity was more drastic and the CEF suspended all payments until June 2018, but the former mayor of Rio de Janeiro, Eduardo Paes, decided to continue the project, reducing their pace. For this, once again public funds should be used. The mayor, three days left before the end of his term, order the municipality to buy R$ 62.5 million of CEPACs to remove the debt with the Concessionary, agreed to receive R$725.9 million in CEPACs as a guarantee to remove future debts and determined payments of up to R$ 219.6 million to the Concessionary with its own resources (*Jornal do Brasil*, 2017b; *Jornal do Comércio*, 2017).

As the mayor Marcelo Crivella, who followed Eduarto Paes in 2017, suspended the payments, the debt with the Porto Novo Concessionary began to grow. In June of 2017, the Concessionary interrupted the services, resulting in the accumulation of trash, the deterioration of squares, roads and gardens (Agência Brasil, 2017). This time, the municipality directly assumed the management of the area and also paid R$ 198 million to the Concessionary to retake the activities (*Diário do Porto*, 2018).

It was expected that in June 2018, after two years of capitalisation, the FIIPM would take-over the routine obligatory disbursements. Nevertheless, in May of the same year, the CEF communicated the lack of resources (*Diário do Porto*, 2018). In June, the Porto Novo Concessionary interrupted once again the works and services. The area stayed without basic trash collection services and maintenance, increasing the sense of abandonment (O Globo, 2018a). The solution appeared only in August, when the CEF and the municipality signed an agreement, according to which the FIIPM would transfer R$ 147 million to the public–private partnership, a value well below the R$ 429 million owed, according to the contract. The CEF also would bring resources originated from the sale of commercial buildings in the region, which were considered to be social buildings, raising R$ 50 million (*IstoÉ Dinheiro*, 2018). With amounts less than expected, the Porto Novo Concessionary would decrease the pace of its activities. The result would supposedly be the non-fulfilling of the deadlines of the Porto Maravilha project, with a long delay of the works and delays in the provision of services.

During the recent years dominated by the crisis both in Brazil and Rio de Janeiro, the unfeasibility of the CEPACs, the instrument created for financing the project Porto Maravilha, has become more and more evident as the interest for the CEPACs remained from far behind the initial expectations (Fundação Getulio Vargas, 2017: 46). This does not have to do with a mere dysfunctionality. Within financial accumulation, interest-bearing capital tends to occupy the centre of the economic and social relations. It occupies an external position to the other forms of capital and it imposes over other logics (Chesnais, 2016: 67 ff). In the case of the Porto Maravilha project, the specific downturn of the port zone real estate market has reaffirmed the process of the CEPACs' overvaluation. Note that their prices do not stop increasing, that is, they do not oscillate according to the offer and demand within the real estate market. As the CEPACs do not find buyers to complete works and ventures, it reinforces its function to the finance accumulation.

Crisis anchored at the port 95

It is then, in truth, a vicious cycle. The low interest for CEPACs for the licensing of new constructions and the contraction of the real estate market lead to the interest for CEPACs for speculative purposes increase. Without resources to enable the public–private partnership, the Porto Novo Concessionary interrupts its activities. Works that could revalorise the space are not carried out; basic services of cleaning and preservation are suspended. Note here that, in the real economy, the crisis at the Port would promote a form of decommodification of the space. At the same time, as seen, the unitary values of the fictitious assets do not stop increasing. The crisis of the Port is, then, a crisis of the overaccumulation of CEPACs, as a result of the contradictory effects of its finance capital for determining the dynamics of other capitals. For compensating the negatives effects of the crises for profit, new expropriations are required. They represent a recommodification of spaces that were uncommodified during the crisis. It takes back, thus, the violence inherent to the project Porto Maravilha.

There is still no news about the new evictions, but the mayor Marcelo Crivella defended in December 2018 the installation of a large casino in the region (O Globo, 2018b), which have been prohibited in Brazil since 1946. Crivella already requested that the President Jair Bolsonaro helps to pass in the National Congress a law that would allow the opening of a casino from the North American Tycoon magnet Sheldon Adelson in the port district of Rio de Janeiro. The mayor wishes a billion dollar venture, the same size of what Adelson constructed in Singapore (O Globo, 2018b). Equally moralist, conservative and religious, the mayor and the president appear to not care at all about their own moral values, which should condemn gambling. They also do not care about the physical, symbolic, cultural, political or aesthetical violence that such a project could unleash. On the contrary, as already seen, this authoritarian violence has been a marking of their administrations as mayor of Rio de Janeiro and as President of Brazil.

Notes

1 In 2008 , when the crisis exploded, the ex-president affirmed that: 'There (in the United States), there is a tsunami;, here, if it even reaches, a little wave will arrive that will not even give a place to ski' (O Globo, 2008).
2 The importance of the question of gender as a nurturing source for the reactions to 'lulismo' and for the electoral victory of Bolsonaro is evident in the very electoral campaign of the candidate and his fight to the exhaustion of what the global right wing movements call 'gender ideology', that is, the affirmation that gender roles are not due to nature, but are social constructions. Qualitative studies such as those developed by Pinheiro-Machado and Scalco (2018:57) demonstrate that, even in the poorest areas, 'the boom of girls that declare themselves feminists' motivates boys to join Bolsonaro as a response to the 'loss of the social protagonism and the feeling of disestablishment of the masculine hegemony'.
3 The State University of Rio de Janeiro turned itself into a symbol of forced precarisation for the acts of the above-described expropriations. Since 2014, the government has constrained its budget by delaying transfers. The situation brought the suspension of maintenance services and a systematic delay of scholarships (including student shareholders). In 2017, the salaries of professors and public technical and administrative employees accumulated five months delayed (Deutsche Welle Brasil, 2017).

Conclusions

Rio de Janeiro's port district represents a space of synthesis which reflects and concretises Brazil's various historical stages of capitalism. The same can be said of the country's various forms of integration into the global economy and different formats of entangled accumulation. The dynamic of integration, disconnection and reconnection of physical spaces and social spheres to the capitalist economy is not only materialised in typical port functions and activities, but also in the port's interaction with its surroundings.

From the perspective of the merchant capitalism, the port was of singular historical relevance, serving as one of the main (for centuries, the only) junctions through which the outflow of internal products, predominantly primary ones, and the influx of imported manufactured goods and enslaved Africans traversed. But that is not all. It is a space which has always facilitated social relations of exchange (of experience, human beings and utilities) between the capitalist world and Brazil as a (post)colonial region marked by, often, non-capitalist economic relations. The port district itself assumed this nodular role in the seizure of non-commodified spaces for the purpose of capitalist expansion. The port and its surroundings have always been expropriated or abandoned to the rhythm of the interests of global accumulation. From this point of view, the port in its different times is not only a means of entangled capitalist expropriations and accumulations in Brazil, but rather becomes a space where such accumulation is reproduced intensely and perpetually.

Created in the 16th century, the port allowed primary goods to leave the colony and industrialised products from the metropolis to enter it, as well as serving as the entry point for a huge contingent (still immeasurable in its entirety) of imprisoned, enslaved and commercialised Africans. But the port not only functioned as the gate of entry and exit for goods and human beings. The space of the port also served as a cemetery for recently arrived Africans in Brazil, a slave market and a place where various services were provided.

The space bordering the port, the port district, has changed its functions in the process of capitalist accumulation. Initially, it was the focal point of activities essential for integrating the colonial economy into global capitalism. Gradually, the surroundings of the port came to be seen as a degraded space within a city growing into and becoming denser in removed areas. The neighbouring areas were increasingly occupied by the poor, freed and later liberated blacks, in

Conclusions 97

addition to destitute migrants from other regions of the country, in particular from the Northeast.

In the second half of the 20th century, as a result of a movement towards decommodification driven by the flow of industrial capital, the port district was seen as a precarious and degraded urban environment, disconnected from capitalist accumulation. The Porto Maravilha project at the beginning of the 21st century thus represented a concerted effort by powerful interests and corporations to incorporate this territory, central but at the time weakly integrated into value production, into the dynamic of – now – finance capitalism. During the political and economic crisis in which Brazil has been emerged since 2014, dynamics of accumulation observed in Rio de Janeiro and specifically in the port area once again illustrate and highlight processes which take place in the whole country. First, the negative effects of the crisis over capitalist profits led the local governments to create new legal – and also illegal – access channels to State resources for investors, as also observed at the federal level. This goes hand in hand with other forms of expropriations such as the use of workers' pension funds for speculative resources, cutting of workers' rights, evictions, etc. To contain reactions against these expropriations, local governments in Rio de Janeiro as well as the Federal Government expand repressive legislations and strengthen the control apparatus of the State. Further mechanisms of disarticulating protest and opponents encompass a political discourse which creates fictive enemies ('communists', 'gays', 'marginals') and disseminates resentments and new social cleavages. This strategy has been extremely successful so far: it led to the election of far-right politicians to occupy the presidency of Brazil and the government of Rio de Janeiro. Once in power, they have been continuously working at both levels expanding spaces within the State for the capital and disarticulating resistances against the same strategy.

In its four centuries of existence, the trajectory of the port embodies the dynamics of entangled capitalist accumulation. Most importantly, the in- and outflow of humans and commodities illustrate the interconnections present between local and global capitalist accumulation, initiated in the colonial period with the export of sugar and the slave trade. Later, the export of gold and coffee and the import of manufactured products became part of this flux. In the 20th century, when the port lost its importance as a corridor of entry and exit for commodities and persons, the links between local and global accumulation largely dissipated, only to be taken up again in the 21st century. This is the point when the Porto Maravilha project sought to reintegrate the physical space of the port into the routes of global tourism and the canals through which financial global capital circulates.

These different historical patterns of incorporating non-commodified spaces into the process of accumulation coexist in these different phases. In this way, for example, the very first order in 1618, which precluded autonomous work in port services, cemented the role of slavery in primitive accumulation, which was, as Marx' put it, accomplished by means of colonisation, robbery and explicit violence. The monopoly over the provision of these services was granted to the concessionaire, a slave owner. The port services catered to the export of colonial

98 *Conclusions*

products, whose incorporated surplus was appropriated in the metropolis and in the commercial flows between the metropolis and other European countries. Due to this, the accumulation facilitated by the port is also the accumulation described by Luxemburg and which insists on decoupling between the spaces of production and appropriation of surplus.

Associated with these processes of commodification of the port space as a whole, a range of regulatory interventions have passed through their function-ends, function-means and interactions with the city, ensuring partnerships between public and private actors as well as the repression and discipline of the labour-power, which was first enslaved and later free.

Public–private partnerships in the broader sense, following the pattern of expropriations, have accompanied the entire history of the port, as is shown by the 1618 order cited above, probably the first public–private partnership in Brazilian history. This is also shown in the concession of the lazarette to the three main slave traders of the period in 1810; the bestowing of the administration of the Cemetery of Pretos Novos upon the Church; and, more recently, the Porto Maravilha project. These partnerships involved multiple associations between political decisions and economic interests, creating a favourable climate for privileges, monopolies and illicit advantages. As such, entangled accumulation interconnects the licit to the illicit, as is shown by the diverse forms of legislation in the different phases of the existence of the port, namely: the favouring of the Governor General's brother in the provision of storage services (1618), the State guaranteed oligopoly of the three biggest slave traders of Rio de Janeiro at that time to provide medical care to recently arrived slaves in quarantine (1810) and the favouring of entrepreneurs and politicians who are today (2018) incarcerated for embezzling public funds in the public–private partnership meant to execute the Porto Maravilha project.

In addition to these partnerships, penal law has made use of violent repressive techniques to adjust the local population and its labour power to the new situation of commodification in all of these phases.

What is more, the history of the port represents a large degree of continuity concerning the combination of public policies, regulatory instruments and the mobilisation of culture and discursive resources as a way of incorporating non-commodified spaces into the accumulation process. Beginning in the 17th century, the State and the law have acted in tandem to implement public works and regimes of concession and private property to guarantee the appropriation of surplus labour and product with port services and its related activities. In the latter case, the different agendas aiming to mechanise and modernise the structure of the port – and Rodrigues Alves' reform, in particular – have always had an ambivalent impact: despite expanding the movement of goods and the flow of tourists, they have destroyed the environment (by means of landfills, disappearance of beaches and hills, etc.) and precarised the labour and housing conditions for the local population.

By implementing these urbanistic reforms and also sanitary mechanisms, the State has configured and continues to configure the dynamics of integration of the port zone as a space where real estate capital is accumulated. This is especially evident in the Pereira Passos Reform and the Porto Maravilha project. Both are examples of urban restructuring which, oriented towards a supposed aesthetic of cleanliness and security, seek to 'beautify' the area by making it more attractive for residence and entertainment for more prosperous social strata.

The interventions made in the context of the Pereira Passos Reform, based specifically on sanitarian justifications, implied the violent repression of the local, mainly Afrodescendent population, whose ways of life supposedly deviated from the mainstream civilisatory model. In the case of Porto Maravilha, the process has gradually become more complex. Following the initial attempt to make invisible the history and cultural heritage that mark the space of the port, it was attempted to ascribe market value to local traditions so as to integrate them into the publicity campaign aiming to enhance the value of the ground and the real estate in the area.

Note that the accumulation of real estate capital in the area is tied to the expropriation of local culture. Starting at the end of the 19th century at the latest, culture has performed a dual function. In the past, Afro-Brazilian cultural manifestations concentrated in the port district were viewed as an expression of moral deterioration of the area and thus used as a pretext for sanitarian and disciplinary intervention by the State. In the contemporary context, these same manifestations serve as an argument for stimulating the integration of the area into the financialised real estate market.

In both cases, the integration of the port district into capitalist accumulation has displaced the local population. When looking at different mayors of Rio de Janeiro, Pereira Passos was only surpassed in the displacement of families by Eduardo Paes, the 'Olympic champion' of removals. Whereas the former expelled 20,000 families between 1902 and 1906, the second removed 20,299 families between January 2009 and December of 2013 alone. Halfway through his tenure, the number of removals carried out by Paes' government exceeded 70,000 (Betim, 2015; Faulhaber and Azevedo, 2015: 16). Although these figures refer to the entire city and not exclusively to the port area, they are quite significant.

In these cases, the contribution of the State has been to commodify the land belonging to the port district; yet at other times, it has acted to decommodify the area by building roads that degraded the local space as well as by investing in other areas of the city, in this way shifting the interests of the real estate market and services away from the port. These processes were unleashed in the course of the 20th century, in particular with the construction of major roads, such as Avenida Presidente Vargas, and viaducts, such as the Perimetral Bridge in 1940–1950. By facilitating rapid transit, they decoupled the port district from a significant part of the population.

Between commodification and decommodification, the State, too, has resorted to the discourse of 'emptiness' and 'degraded areas' throughout history in order to devalorise the area and, in turn, permit its incorporation into accumulation at a low cost. These discourses are carriers of symbolic violence in that they have unleashed actions that conceal and erase the memory inscribed in the area. They have sought to invisibilise people, resistance, practices and social experiences in order to devalorise them and, by doing so render them an easy object

100   *Conclusions*

of expropriation. In the 19th century, the Imperatriz Wharf buried the Valongo Wharf to keep it out of the sight of the Queen of the Two Sicilies, the new empress of Brazil. Likewise, the Museum of Tomorrow (with its aim to explore the future) shocks any immanent and transcendent meaning contained in the history of the area, which is both the synthesis of Brazilian history and a miniature of the history of global capitalist accumulation.

Finally, as far as entangled accumulation and the interpenetration of social categories are concerned, it is clear that the integration of the non-capitalist space of the colony into the global dynamic of capitalism was concomitant with the construction of the concept of race and the enslavement of black human beings captured in Africa. At the same time, the port functioned as a port of entry for enslaved blacks as well as a fundamental link in the long chain that transformed the life of the enslaved into a ware. While slaves were traded for goods in the African ports, they were traded for money in the port of Rio de Janeiro, thus allowing the trader to make profits. Before being traded, slaves were classified, polished and put on display. Following the prohibition of the trade of enslaved Africans and especially after the abolition of slavery in 1888, a small number of ex-slaves were incorporated into the port services as a class of wage labourers. A significant proportion of them was not integrated into the labour market or were only integrated precariously. It is they who tried to settle in the devalorised territory on the outskirts of the port, resisting all attempts at removal and economic and political violence, past and present.

Bibliography

ABRATEC (2016) Estatísticas. Available at: http://www.abratec-terminais.org.br/estatisticas (accessed 8 February 2016).

ADEMIRJ (2012) Revitalização da zona portuária impulsiona mercado imobiliário. Available at: http://www.ademi.org.br/article.php3?id_article=48381 (accessed 22 January 2018).

Agência Brasil (2017) Concessionária suspende serviços na zona portuária do Rio por falta de pagamento, July 04. Available at: http://agenciabrasil.ebc.com.br/geral/noticia/2017-07/concessionaria-suspende-servicos-na-zona-portuaria-do-rio-por-falta-de (accessed 8 February 2018).

Alencastro L. F. (1997) Vida privada e ordem privada no Império. In: Alencastro L. F. (ed) *História da vida privada no Brasil*, Vol. 2. São Paulo: Cia das Letras, pp. 11–94.

Almeida G. R. (2013) Uma maravilha de capital. *Anais do XXVII Simpósio Nacional de História*. ANPUH Natal.

Altvater E. (2010) *Der große Krach: oder die Jahrhundertkrise von Wirtschaft und Finanzen von Politik und Natur*. Münster: Westfälisches Dampfboot.

Andreatta V. and Herce Vallejo M. (2011) Y Las Olimpíadas de 2016: La revitalizacion del centro urbano sobre la conjugación de los proyectos 'Porto Maravilha'. In 'Porto Olimpico'. *Cuaderno Urbano* 10(10): 127–155.

Araujo K. (2016) *El miedo a los subordinados: Una teoría de la autoridade*. Santiago: LoM.

Arraes J. and Silva A. (2014) Porto Maravilha: Continuities and changes. Available at: https://portomaravilha.com.br/continuities_and_changes (accessed 22 January 2018).

Assumpção E. and Schramm F. R. (2013) Bioética e habitação: leitura ética sobre as ocupações urbanas no centro do Rio de Janeiro. *Revista bioética* 21(1): 96–105.

Azevedo A. N. (2003) A reforma Pereira Passos: uma tentativa de integração urbana. *Revista Rio de Janeiro* 10: 33–79.

Backhouse M. (2015) *Grüne Landnahme – Palmölexpansion und Landkonflikte in Amazonien*. Münster: Westfälisches Dampfboot.

Backhouse M., Baquero J. and Costa S. (2016) Between rights and power asymmetries: Contemporary struggles for land in Brazil and Colombia. In: Fischer-Lescano A. and Möller K. (eds) *Transnationalisation of Social Rights*. Cambridge/Antwerp/Portland: Intersentia, pp. 239–264.

BBC Brasil (2016a) 4 motivos que levaram o Rio a decretar estado de calamidade pública, June 18. Available at: https://www.bbc.com/portuguese/brasil-36566996 (accessed 10 March 2018).

102 *Bibliography*

BBC Brasil (2016b) 'Cedemos casa para festa mas não fomos convidados': quatro contrastes no Rio da Olimpíada, August 04. Available at: https://www.bbc.com/portuguese/brasil-36975679 (accessed 10 March 2018).

Benchimol J. L. (1992) *Pereira Passos: Um Haussmann Tropical*. Rio de Janeiro: Prefeitura da Cidade do Rio de Janeiro.

Betin F. (2015) Remoções na Vila Autódromo expõem o lado B das Olimpíadas do Rio. *El Pais*. Available at: https://brasil.elpais.com/brasil/2015/06/20/politica/1434753946_363539.html (accessed 22 January 2018).

Bicalho M. F. (2007) *O Rio de Janeiro: uma capital entre dois impérios*. Rio de Janeiro: Arquivo Geral da Cidade do Rio de Janeiro.

Bird J. (1957) *The Geography of the Port of London*. London: Hutchinson University Library.

Blackburn R. (1997) *The Making of New World Slavery: From the Baroque to the Modern 1492–1800*. London: Verso.

BM&FBOVESPA (2015) Certificado de Potencial Adicional de Construção. Available at: http://www.bmfbovespa.com.br/pt-br/mercados/fundos/cepacs/cepacs.aspx?idioma=pt-br (accessed 8 February 2016).

Boechat C. A., Pitta F. T. and Toledo C. A. (2017) Land Grabbing e crise do capital: possíveis intersecções dos debates. *GEOgraphia* 19(40): 75–91.

Boltanski L. and Chiapello E. (2005) *The New Spirit of Capitalism*. London: Verso.

Borras S., Kay C., Gómez S. and Wilkinson J. (2012) Land grabbing and global capitalist accumulation: Key features in Latin America. *Canadian Journal of Development Studies/Revue canadienne d'études du développement* 33(4: Land Grabbing in Latin America): 402–416.

Boyer R. and Saillard Y. (eds) (2005) *Regulation Theory: The State of the Art*. London: Routledge.

Brasil Econômico (2012) Investimento de R$ 7 bilhões muda a face do Porto do Rio, November 13. Available at: http://www.ademi.org.br/article.php3?id_article=51030 (accessed 10 March 2018).

Bringel B. and Pleyers G. (eds) (2017) *Protesta e indignación global: Los movimientos sociales en el nuevo orden mundial*. Buenos Aires: Clacso/Rio de Janeiro.

Burbank M., Andranovich G. and Heying C. H. (2001) *Olympic Dreams: The Impact of Mega-Events on Local Politics*. London: Lynne Rienner.

Caldeira J. (2011) O processo econômico. In: Silva A. C. (ed) *Crise colonial e independência 1808–1830*. Madrid/Rio de Janeiro: Fundación Mapfre/Objetiva, pp. 161–204.

Cano W. (2015) Crise e industrialização no Brasil entre 1929 e 1954: a reconstrução do Estado Nacional e a política nacional de desenvolvimento. *Revista de Economia Política* 35(3): 444–460.

Cano W. (2017) Brasil – construção e desconstrução do desenvolvimento. *Economia e Sociedade* 26(2): 265–302.

Cardoso E. D., Vaz L. V. and Albernaz M. P. (1987) *Saúde, Gamboa, Santo Cristo*. Rio de Janeiro: Index.

Cardoso R. (2015) From Valongo to Favela: Brazil's First Periphery. In: Diniz C. and Cardoso R. (eds) *From Valongo to Favela: The Imaginary and the Periphery*. Rio de Janeiro: Instituto Odeon, pp. 181–188 (bilingual edition).

Carta Capital (2016) Após 11 meses de processo, Câmara cassa Eduardo Cunha por 450 votos a 10. Available at: https://www.cartacapital.com.br/politica/apos-11-meses-de-processo-camara-cassa-eduardo-cunha-por-450-votos-a-10 (accessed 22 January 2018).

Bibliography   103

Carta Capital (2017) A crise do Rio de Janeiro e o golpe de 2016, November 16. Available at: https://www.cartacapital.com.br/blogs/brasil-debate/a-crise-do-rio-e-o-golpe-de-2016 (accessed 10 March 2018).

de Carvalho J. M. (2007) Prefácio. In: da Silva Pereira J. C. M. (ed) *À flor da terra: o cemitério dos pretos novos no Rio de Janeiro*. Rio de Janeiro: IPHAN.

Carvalho L. (2019) Gabinete do crime. *Folha de São Paulo*, January 24. Available at: https://www1.folha.uol.com.br/colunas/laura-carvalho/2019/01/gabinete-do-crime. shtml (accessed 10 March 2018).

Castro F. A. (2014) *Imposto de renda da pessoa física: Comparações internacionais Medidas de progressividade e redistribuição*. Brasília: Universidade de Brasília, Master thesis.

Cesec (2019) *Intervenção federal: um modelo para não copiar*. Rio de Janeiro: Observatório da Intervenção. Available at: https://drive.google.com/file/d/1UPulZi6XpsK8DQo6c5o VmwUFUhypkOpA/view (accessed 10 March 2018).

Chalhoub S. (1996) *Cidade febril: cortiços e epidemias na Corte Imperial*. São Paulo: Companhia das Letras.

Chesnais F. (2016) *Finance Capital Today: Corporations and Banks in the Lasting Global Slump*. Leiden/Boston: Brill.

CEPAL (2019) *Panorama Social de América Latina 2018*. Santiago: Comisión Económica para América Latina y el Caribe.

Cislaghi J. F. (2017) Apropriação privada de fundo público por meio do gasto tributário no estado do Rio de Janeiro. *Revista ADvir (ASDUERJ)* 36(1): 149–158.

Cislaghi J. F., Souza T., Perez A. A., Silva T. B., Garcia L. F. and Santos M. C. C. (2016) Crise do capital e suas consequências no Brasil: o caso do estado do Rio de Janeiro. Anais do XV Congresso Brasileiro de *Assistentes* Sociais, Olinda.

Comitê Popular da Copa and Olímpiadas do Rio de Janeiro (2015) Olímpiada Rio 2016 os jogos da exclusão. *Dossiê Megaeventos e violações dos direitos humanos no Rio de Janeiro (novembro)*. Rio de Janeiro.

Conrad S. and Randeria S. (2002) Einleitung. Geteilte Geschichten. Europa in einer postkolonialen Welt. In: Conrad S. and Randeria S. (eds) *Jenseits des Eurozentrismus: Postkoloniale Perspektiven in den Geschichts- und Kulturwissenschaften*. Frankfurt am Main: Campus, pp. 9–49.

Costa H. (2000) *100 anos de carnaval no Rio de Janeiro*. São Paulo: Irmãos Vitale.

Costa S. and Motta R. C. (2019) Social classes and the far right in Brazil. In: Esteves P. and Foley C. (eds) *In Spite of You: Bolsonaro and the New Brazilian Resistance*. London: OR Books, pp. 103–116.

da Costa Cardoso I. C. (2013) O papel da Operação Urbana Consorciada do Porto do Rio de Janeiro na estruturação do espaço urbano: uma "máquina de crescimento urbano"? *O Social em Questão* 29: 69–100.

da Costa Silva A. (2011a) As Marcas do Período. In: da Costa Silva A. (ed) *Crise Colonial e Independência 1808–1830*. Madrid/Rio de Janeiro: Fundación Mapfre/Objetiva, pp. 23–34.

da Costa Silva A. (2011b) População e Sociedade. In: da Costa Silva A. (ed) *Crise Colonial e Independência 1808–1830*. Madrid/Rio de Janeiro: Fundación Mapfre/Objetiva, pp. 35–74.

Couper A. (1972) *The Geography of Sea Transport*. London: Hutchinson.

CPI do Porto Maravilha (2017). Available at: https://cpiportomaravilha.com/ (accessed 22 January 2018).

104 *Bibliography*

Da Silva D. A. (2012) *O enigma da capital: a mudança do vice-reinado para o Rio de Janeiro em 1763*. Doutorado, Rio de Janeiro: Universidade de São Paulo.

Darwin C. (1959 [1913]) *The Voyage of the Beagle*. Tadworth: The Press of Kingswood.

De Paula L. F. and Pires M. (2017) Crise e perspectivas para a economia brasileira. *Estudos Avançados* 31(89): 125–144.

Deutsche Welle Brasil (2016) *Como o estado do Rio de Janeiro chegou à falência?* June 20. Available at: https://www.dw.com/pt-br/como-o-estado-do-rio-de-janeiro-chegou-%C3%A0-fal%C3%AAncia/a-19344065 (accessed 10 March 2018).

Deutsche Welle Brasil (2017) Um símbolo da falência do Rio. January 31. Available at: https://www.dw.com/pt-br/um-s%C3%ADmbolo-da-fal%C3%AAncia-do-rio/a-37351577 (accessed 10 March 2018).

Diário do Porto (2018) *Porto Maravilha em crise: o futuro nas mãos da Caixa*. June 07. Available at: https://diariodoporto.combr/porto-maravilha-em-crise-o-futuro-nas-maos-da-caixa/ (accessed 10 March 2018).

DIEESE (2017) *Balanço das greves de 2016*. São Paulo: Estudos e Pesquisas. Available at: https://www.dieese.org.br/balancodasgreves/2016/estPesq84balancogreves2016.html (accessed 22 January 2018).

Dörre K. (2015) The new Landnahme: Dynamics and limits of financial market capitalism. In: Dörre K., Lessenich S. and Rosa H. (eds) *Sociology, Capitalism, Critique*. London: Verso.

Dörre K. and Holst H. (2010) Einschätzungen zum Forschungsstand Prekarität. In: IG MetalL (ed) *Beiträge zur Arbeitspolitik und Arbeitsforschung Handlungsfelder Forschungsstände Aufgaben*. Frankfurt am Main: IG Metall, pp. 32–43.

Ducruet C. (2006) Dynamiques scalaires et temporelles des villes-ports: typologie mondiale de 330 trajectoires urbano-portuaires, 1990–2000. *Actes des Rencontres de Theoquant*. Available at: http://thema.univ-fcomte.fr/theoq/pdf/2005/TQ2005%20ARTICLE%206.pdf (accessed 22 January 2018).

Ekman M. (2012) Understanding accumulation: The relevance of Marx's theory of primitive accumulation in media and communication studies. *Triple C, Communication, Capitalism & Critique* 10(2): 156–170.

El Pais (2016a) Rio de Janeiro da euforia à depressão. Available at: https://brasil.elpais.com/brasil/2016/11/10/politica/1478799785_114849.html (accessed 10 March 2018).

El Pais (2016b) Em plena crise de segurança policiais ameaçam colocar o Rio em xeque. Available at: https://brasil.elpais.com/brasil/2016/11/09/politica/1478647673_736846.html (accessed 10 March 2018).

El Pais (2017) A tragédia do Rio do pódio à lama: 'Estamos sofrendo mas continuaremos gritando'. Available at: https://brasil.elpais.com/brasil/2017/07/16/politica/15002223 36_134535.html (accessed 10 March 2018).

El Pais (2019) Marielle assombra Flávio Bolsonaro mais morta do que viva. Available at: https://brasil.elpais.com/brasil/2019/01/24/opinion/1548366291_877712.html (accessed 10 March 2018).

Fairweather C. (2017) The sharing economy as primitive accumulation: Locating the political-economic position of the capital-extractive sharing economy. *HPS: The Journal of History & Political Science* 5: 51–63.

Faulhaber L. and Azevedo L. (2015) *SMH 2016 : remoções no Rio de Janeiro Olímpico*. Rio de Janeiro: Mórula.

Figueiredo C. (2005) *O Porto e a Cidade: O Rio de Janeiro entre 1965 e 1910*. Rio de Janeiro: Casa da Palavra.

Fine B. (2010) Locating financialisation. *Historical Materialism* 18(2): 97–116.

Bibliography 105

Florentino M. (2014) *Em Costas Negras. Uma História do Tráfico de Escravos entre a África e o Rio de Janeiro (Séculos XVIII e XIX)*. São Paulo: UNESP.

Folha de São Paulo (2016) Vitrine de Paes, Porto Maravilha teve propina, indicam e-mails. Available at: http://www1.folha.uol.com.br/esporte/olimpiada-no-rio/2016/03/1752753-vitrine-de-paes-porto-maravilha-teve-propina-indicam-e-mails.shtml (accessed 7 January 2018).

Fonseca P. C. and Salomão I. C. (2017) Industrialização brasileira: notas sobre o debate historiográfico. *Tempo* 23(1): 86–104.

da Fonseca R. M. (2005) A Lei de Terras e o advento da propriedade moderna no Brasil. *Anuario Mexicano de Historia del Derecho* 17: 97–112.

Fontes V. (2010) *O Brasil e o capital-imperialismo: teoria e história*. Rio de Janeiro: Editora UFRJ.

Fontes V. (2017) David Harvey: Dispossession or Expropriation? Does capital have an "outside"? *Revista Direito e Praxis* 8(3): 2199–2211.

Franco M. S. C. (1969 [1999]) *Homens livres na ordem escravocrata*. São Paulo: Unesp.

Frank, A. G. (1978) *World Accumulation, 1492–1789*. Basingstoke: Palgrave Macmillan.

Fridman F. (1999) *Donos do Rio em Nome do Rei. Uma história fundiária da cidade do Rio de Janeiro*. Rio de Janeiro: Zahar Garamond.

Fundação Getulio Vargas (2017) *O Rio em perspectiva: um diagnóstico de escolhas públicas*. Rio de Janeiro: FGV/DAAP.

Furtado C. (1967 [1959]) *Formação Econômica do Brasil*, 7ª ed. São Paulo: Cia Ed. Nacional.

G1 (2015) Rio terá Boulevard Olímpico com eventos e transmissões de jogos. Available at: http://g1.globo.com/rio-de-janeiro/noticia/2015/06/rio-tera-boulevard-olimpico-com-eventos-e-transmissoes-dos-jogos.html (accessed 12 February 2016).

G1 (2016) Servidores de 33 categorias do estado do RJ estão em greve. Available at: http://g1.globo.com/rio-de-janeiro/noticia/2016/04/servidores-de-33-categorias-do-estado-do-rj-estao-em-grevEhtml (accessed 10 March 2018).

G1 (2017a) Alerj aprova aumento da contribuição previdenciária. Available at: https://g1.globo.com/rio-de-janeiro/noticia/picciani-reaparece-na-alerj-em-dia-de-votacao-do-aumento-da-contribuicao-previdenciaria.ghtml (accessed 10 March 2018).

G1 (2017b) Acordo da União com o RJ prevê ajuste fiscal de R\$ 63 bilhões até 2020. Available at: https://g1.globo.com/rio-de-janeiro/noticia/acordo-da-uniao-com-o-rj-preve-ajuste-de-r-63-bilhoes-ate-2020.ghtml (accessed 10 March 2018).

G1 (2018a) Decisão do ministro Marco Aurélio Mello não afeta prisões de Cabral Cunha e Pezão dizem defesas. Available at: https://g1.globo.com/rj/rio-de-janeiro/noticia/2018/12/19/decisao-do-ministro-marco-aurelio-mello-nao-afeta-prisao-de-pezao-diz-defesa.ghtml (accessed 10 March 2018).

G1 (2018b) MPF diz que Pezão operava esquema de corrupção próprio e recebeu mais de R\$ 39 milhões entre 2007 e 2015. Available at: https://g1.globo.com/rj/rio-de-janeiro/noticia/2018/11/29/mpf-diz-que-pezao-operava-esquema-de-corrupcao-proprio-e-recebeu-mais-de-r-25-milhoes-entre-2007-e-2015.ghtml (accessed 10 March 2018).

G1 (2018c) MP entra com ação contra Pezão e Dornelles por corrupção em isenções. Available at: https://g1.globo.com/rj/rio-de-janeiro/noticia/2018/12/19/mp-entra-com-acao-contra-pezao-e-dornelles-por-corrupcao-em-isencoes.ghtml (accessed 10 March 2018).

Gaffney C. (2010) Mega-events and socio-spatial dynamics in Rio de Janeiro, 1919–2016. *Journal of Latin American Geography* 9(1): 7–29.

106 Bibliography

da Gama Silva Werneck M., Novaes P. R. and dos Santos Junior O. A. (2018) *A estagnação da dinâmica imobiliária e a crise da operação urbana do Porto Maravilha.* Rio de Janeiro: Informe Crítico/IPPUR-UFRJ.

Gerstenberger D. (2015) Europe in the Tropics? The transfer of the Portuguese Royal Court to Brazil (1807/8) and the adaptation of European ideals in the new imperial capital. *Comparativ* 25(3/4): 36–50.

Gileno C. H. (2007) A legislação indígena: ambigüidades na formação do Estado-nação no Brasil. *Caderno CRH* 20(49): 123–133.

Gonçalves G. L. (2017) Kapitalistische Landnahme: Eine Erweiterung der kritischen Rechtssoziologie. *Working Paper der DFG -Kollegforscher_innengruppe Postwachstumsgesellschaften* 4: 1–35.

Gonçalves G. L. (2018) Capitalist Landnahme: A New Marxist Approach to Law. *Global Dialogue – Magazine of the International Sociological Association* 8: 40–42.

Gonçalves G. L. and Machado M. R. A. (2018) Neoliberalismo autoritário em cinco atos: do salvamento de bancos à morte de Marielle. *Le Monde Diplomatique (Brasil)* 11(129): 22–24.

Góngora-Mera M. (2017) Transregional articulations of law and race in Latin America: A legal genealogy of inequality. In: Jelin E. et al. (ed) *Global Entangled Inequalities: Conceptual Debates and Evidence from Latin America.* Abingdon: Routledge, pp. 42–58.

Gorender J. (1978) *O escravismo colonial.* São Paulo: Ática.

Haag C. (2011) Os ossos que falam. *Revista Pesquisa FAPESP* 190: 24–29.

Habermas J. (1973) *Legitimationsprobleme im Spätkapitalismus.* Frankfurt: Suhrkamp

Harvey D. (1975) The geography of capitalist accumulation: A reconstruction of the Marxian theory. *Antipode* 7(2): 9–21.

Harvey D. (1985) The geopolitics of capitalism. In: Gregory D. and Urry J. (eds) *Social Relations and Spatial Structure.* London: Macmillan, pp. 128–163.

Harvey D. (1989) From managerialism to entrepreneurialism: The transformation in urban governance in late capitalism. *Geografiska Annaler* 71(1): 3–17.

Harvey D. (2002) The art of rent: Globalization, monopoly and the commodification of culture. *Socialist Register* 38: 93–110.

Harvey D. (2004) The 'New' imperialism: Accumulation by dispossession. *Socialist Register* 40(40): 63–87.

Harvey D. (2005) *Der neue Imperialismus.* Hamburg: VSA-Verl.

Harvey D. (2006) Neoliberalism as Creative Destruction. *Geografiska Annaler, Serie B,* 88(2): 145–158.

Harvey D. (2010) *The Enigma of Capital and the Crises of Capitalism.* Oxford/New York: Oxford University Press.

Haubner T. (2015) Der Proletarier ist tot, es lebe die Hausfrau? *Marxistischer Feminismus* 34. Available at: http://kritisch- lesen.de/c/1241 (accessed 11 April 2016)

Hilf S. (2012) *Unternehmerische Stadtpolitik in Rio de Janeiro – untersucht am Beispiel des Hafenrevitalisierungsprojekts Porto Maravilha.* Mag.rer.nat. Wien: Universität Wien.

Hilling D. (1988) Socio-economic change in the maritime quarter: The demise of sailortown. In: Hovle B. S., Pinder D. A. and Husain M. S. (eds) *Revitalising the Waterfront: International Dimensions of Dockland Redevelopment.* London: Belhaven Press.

de Honorato C. P. (2008) *Valongo: o mercado de escravos do Rio de Janeiro, 1758–1831.* Mestrado, Rio de Janeiro: Universidade Federal Fluminense.

Bibliography 107

de Honorato C. P. (2006) Controle sanitário dos negros novos no Valongo. *Rio de Janeiro*: *XII Encontro Regional de História*. ANPUH-RJ.

Império do Brasil (1850) Lei 581. Available at: http://www.planalto.gov.br/ccivil_03/leis/lim/lim581.htm (accessed 22 January 2018).

Innis H. (1956) *Essays in Canadian Economic History*. Toronto: University of Toronto Press.

IstoÉ Dinheiro (2018) Com acordo entre Caixa e prefeitura concessionária volta a gerir Porto Maravilha. Available at: https://www.istoedinheiro.com.br/com-acordo-entre-cai xa-e-prefeitura-concessionaria-volta-a-gerir-porto-maravilha/ (accessed 10 March 2019).

Jelin, E., Motta, R. M. and Costa, S. (2017) *Global Entangled Inequalities: Conceptual Debates and Evidence from Latin America*. Abingdon: Routledge.

Johnson A. M. C. (2010) *Sentencing Canudos: Subalternity in the Backlands of Brazil*. Pittsburgh: University of Pittsburgh Press.

Jornal do Brasil (2017a) Porto Maravilha: o fracasso de um projeto bilionário que excluiu os menos favorecidos. Available at: https://www.jb.com.br/redirect.php?url=/rio/noticias/2017/06/04/porto-maravilha-o-fracasso-de-um-projeto-bilionario-que-excluiu-os-menos-favorecidos/ (accessed 10 March 2018).

Jornal do Brasil (2017b) Em nota oficial Prefeitura do Rio confirma reportagem do 'JB' sobre Porto Maravilha, June 27. Available at: https://www.jb.com.br/index.php?id=/acervo/materia.php&cd_matia=924239&dinamico=1&preview=1 (accessed 10 March 2018).

Jornal do Comércio (2017) Zona portuária do Rio de Janeiro vive nó financeiro. Available at: https://www.jornaldocomercio.com/_conteudo/2017/04/cadernos/jc_logistica/5594 77-zona-portuaria-do-rio-de-janeiro-vive-no-financeiro.html (accessed 10 March 2018).

Knox R. (2013) Race, war and international law. *Cambridge Review of International Affairs* 26(1):111–32.

Kotz D. (2009) The financial and economic crisis of 2008. *Review of Radical Political Economics* 41(3): 305–317.

de Lamarão S. T. N. (2006) *Dos Trapiches ao porto: um estudo sobre a área portuária do Rio de Janeiro*. Rio de Janeiro: Secretaria Municipal das Culturas.

Lapavitsas C. (2014) *Profiting Without Producing: How Finance Exploits Us All*. London/New York: Verso.

Lavinas L. (2017) *The Takeover of Social Policy by Financialization: The Brazilian Paradox*. Hampshire: Palgrave.

Lavinas L. and Gonçalves G. L. (2018) Brasil 2018: direitização das classes médias e polarização social. *Le Monde Diplomatique (Brasil)*. Available at: https://diplomatique.org.br/brasil-2018-direitizacao-das-classes-medias-e-polarizacao-social/ (accessed 22 January 2018).

Leopoldi M. A. P. (2000) *Política e Interesses na industrialização brasileira*. São Paulo: Paz e Terra.

Lessa C. (2000) *O Rio de todos os BrasiS Uma reflexão em busca de auto-estima*. Rio de Janeiro: Record.

Lima T. A., Sene G. M. and de Souza M. A. T. (2016) Em busca do Cais do Valongo, Rio de Janeiro, século XIX. *Anais do Museu Paulista: História e Cultura Material, São Paulo* 24(1): 299–391.

Londoño, E. (2017) Brazil's gateway for slaves, now a world heritage site. *New York Times*, 15 July 2017.

Luxemburg R. (2003 [1913]) *The Accumulation of Capital*. London/New York: Routledge Classics.

Marini R. M. (1967) *Subdesarrollo y revolución*. México D. F.: Siglo Veintuno.

108 Bibliography

Marx K. (1906 [1867]) *Capital: A Critique of Political Economy*, Vol. 1. New York: The Modern Library.

Marx K. (1983 [1894]) *Das Kapital: Kritik der politischen Oekonomie*, Vol. 3. Berlin: Dietz.

de Mello F. F. (2003) *A Zona Portuária do Rio de Janeiro: antecedentes e perspectivas*. Mestrado, Rio de Janeiro: Instituto de Pesquisa e Planejamento Urbano e Regional da Universidade Federal do Rio de Janeiro.

Mercês G. and Freire N. (2017) Crise fiscal dos estados e o caso do rio de Janeiro. *Revista GeoUerj* 31(1): 64–80.

Moreira C. C. (2004) *A cidade contemporânea entre a tábula rasa e a preservação*. São Paulo: UNESP.

Moura R. (1995) *Tia Ciata e a Pequena África no Rio de Janeiro*. Rio de Janeiro: Secretária Municipal de Cultura.

Museu do Amanha (2015) Sobre o museu. Available at: https://museudoamanha.org.br/en/about-the-museum (accessed 22 January 2018).

do Nascimento A. P. (2008) *Cidadania, Cor e Disciplina na Revolta dos Marinheiros de 1910*. Rio de Janeiro: Mauad.

Neto A. (2013) Os Cepacs deram certo? *Infraestrutura urbana* 33. Available at: http://infraestruturaurbana17.pini.com.br/solucoes-tecnicas/33/os-cepacs-deram-certo-rio-avanca-em-projetos-financiados-301395-1.aspx (accessed 22 January 2018).

Nogueira I. (2011) Caixa arremata por R$ 3,5 bi todos os títulos do porto do Rio. *Folha de São Paulo*. Available at: https://www1.folha.uol.com.br/fsp/mercado/me1406201107.htm (accessed 22 January 2018).

Norcliffe G., Basset K. and Hoare T. (1996) The emergence of postmodernism on the urban waterfront. Geographical perspectives on changing relationships. *Journal of Transport Geography* 4(2): 123–134.

Noronha G. (2017) Os caminhos cruzados da Grécia e do Rio de Janeiro. Brasil Debate 21 de fevereiro. Available at: https://dev.cartacapital.com.br/blogs/brasil-debate/os-caminhos-cruzados-da-grecia-e-do-rio-de-janeiro/ (accessed 22 January 2018).

de Noronha Santos F. A. (1965) *As freguesias do Rio antigo vistas por Noronha Santos*. Rio de Janeiro: O Cruzeiro.

Nunes A. J. A. (2015) Crónica em tempo de guerra. *Revista Fórum de Direito Financeiro e Econômico* 4(7): 11–30.

Offe C. (1983) Competitive party democracy and the Keynesian Welfare State: Factors of stability and disorganization. *Policy Sciences* 15: 225–246.

O Globo (2008) Lula: crise é tsunami nos EUA e se chegar ao Brasil será 'marolinha'. Available at: https://oglobo.globo.com/economia/lula-crise-tsunami-nos-eua-se-chegar-ao-brasil-sera-marolinha-3827410 (accessed 22 January 2018).

O Globo (2011) Consórcio assume responsabilidade por serviços públicos em parte da Zona Portuária. Available at: https://oglobo.globo.com/rio/consorcio-assume-responsabilidade-por-servicos-publicos-em-parte-da-zona-portuaria-2876145 (accessed 22 January 2018).

O Globo (2013) Paes quer que árbitros e jornalistas fiquem na Barra nos Jogos de 2016. Available at: http://oglobo.globo.com/rio/paes-quer-que-arbitros-jornalistas-fiquem-na-barra-nos-jogos-de-2016-11877405 (accessed 12 February 2016)

O Globo (2015) Rio é segunda maior economia mas indústria é apenas sexta do Brasil. Available at: https://oglobo.globo.com/economia/rio-segunda-maior-economia-mas-industria-apenas-sexta-do-brasil-18233605 (accessed 22 January 2018).

O Globo (2017a) Concessionária Porto Novo reassume administração do Porto Maravilha. Available at: https://oglobo.globo.com/rio/concessionaria-porto-novo-

Bibliography 109

reassume-administracao-do-porto-maravilha-22071277#ixzz54wEVbqtCstest (accessed 22 January 2018)

O Globo (2017b) 'São arruaceiros que querem o tumulto' afirma Pezão sobre protesto na Alerj. Available at: https://oglobo.globo.com/rio/sao-arruaceiros-que-querem-tumulto-afirma-pezao-sobre-protesto-na-alerj-20901413 (accessed 22 January 2018).

O Globo (2018a) Concessionária deixa gestão do Porto Maravilha que sofre sem manutenção. Available at: https://oglobo.globo.com/rio/concessionaria-deixa-gestao-do-porto-maravilha-que-sofre-sem-manutencao-22826379 (accessed 10 March 2018).

O Globo (2018b) Crivella sobre cassino no Porto: 'Sou contra o vício mas contra a miséria e o desemprego'. Available at: https://oglobo.globo.com/rio/crivella-sobre-cassino-no-porto-sou-contra-vicio-mas-contra-miseria-o-desemprego-23310481 (accessed 10 March 2018).

de Oliveira A. and Rodrigues A. (2009) Industrialização na periferia metropolitana do Rio de Janeiro: novos paradigmas para velhos problemas. *Semestre Económico* 12(24 Edición especial): 127–143.

de Oliveira F. (1972) A economia brasileira: crítica à razão dualista. *Novos Estudos Cebrap* 2: 4–82.

O'Rourke K. H. and Williamson J. G. (1999) *Globalization and History: The Evolution of a Nineteenth-Century Atlantic Economy*. Cambridge: MIT Press.

Paes E. (2015) De volta ao centro. *Revista Porto Maravilha* 18: 3.

Pereira L. (2002) *As barricadas da Saúde: Vacina e protesto popular no Rio de Janeiro da Primeira República*. São Paulo: Fundação Perseu Abramo.

Pereira-Machado R. and Scalco L. M. (2018) Da esperança ao ódio: a juventude periférica bolsonarista. In: Gallego E. G. (eds) *O ódio como política. A reinvenção das direitos no Brasil*. São Paulo: Boitempo, pp. 53–60.

Picciotto S. (2011) *Regulating Global Corporate Capitalism*. Cambridge: Cambridge University Press.

Pijning E. (2001) Contrabando, ilegalidade e medidas políticas no Rio de Janeiro do século XVII. *Revista Brasileira de História* 21(42): 397–414.

Pinheiro A. I. F. and de Carvalho Elias Rabha N. M. (2004) *Porto do Rio de Janeiro: Construindo a Modernidade*. Rio de Janeiro: Andrea Jacobsson Estúdio.

Porto Maravilha (2011) Porto Maravilha. Available at: http://portomaravilha.com.br/portomaravilha (accessed 22 January 2018).

Porto Maravilha (2013) Entenda o negócio. Available at: http://www.portomaravilha.com.br/noticiasdetalhe/3981 (accessed 7 January 2018).

Porto Maravilha (2016) Boulevard Olímpico – cerimônia de abertura. Available at: http://www.portomaravilha.com.br/eventosdetalhe/cod/541 (accessed 22 January 2018).

Porto Maravilha (2018) Folder Porto Cultural. Available at: http://www.portomaravilha.com.br/images/pmcul.pdf (accessed 30 January 2018).

Porto Novo (2010) Estrutura acionária. Available at: http://www.portonovosa.com/pt-br/estrutura-acionaria (accessed 22 January 2018).

Porto Novo (2017a) Nota Oficial da Concessionária Porto Novo. Available at: http://www.portonovosa.com/pt-br/noticias/nota-oficial-concessionaria-porto-novo (accessed 22 January 2018).

Prado Júnior C. (1986 [1945]) *História econômica do Brasil*, 33ª. ed. São Paulo: Brasiliense.

PSL (2018) *O caminho da prosperidade Proposta de Plano de Governo*. Brasília: Partido Social Liberal.

110 Bibliography

Pública (2018) Porto Maravilha corre o risco de parar novamente em 2018. Available at: https://apublica.org/2018/02/porto-maravilha-corre-o-risco-de-parar-novamente-em-2018/ (accessed 10 March 2018).

Rainha F. A. and Fonseca P. R. (2013) Morro da Providência e Porto Maravilha: caminhando entre a realidade e a ilegalidade jurídica. In: XV Encontro da Associação Nacional de Pós-Graduação e Pesquisa em Planejamento Urbano e Regional, Recife.

Ramos S. (2019) O que aprendemos com a intervenção. In: *Cesec Intervenção federal: um modelo para não copiar*. Rio de Janeiro: Observatório da Intervenção, pp. 32–35.

Rediker M. (2007) *The Slave Ship: A Human History*. London: John Murray.

Relatório Reservado (2012) Título sem fundo. Available at: https://relatorioreservado.com.br/assunto/porto-maravilha/ (accessed 10 March 2018).

Relatório Reservado (2013a) Tishman Speyer finca suas pilastras no Porto do Rio. Available at: https://relatorioreservado.com.br/assunto/tishman-speyer/ (accessed 10 March 2018).

Relatório Reservado (2013b) Trump in Rio. Available at: https://relatorioreservado.com.br/assunto/porto-maravilha/ (accessed 10 March 2018).

Relatório Reservado (2013c) Maravilha? Available at: https://relatorioreservado.com.br/assunto/porto-maravilha/ (accessed 10 March 2018).

Relatório Reservado (2014a) Salamanca. Available at: https://relatorioreservado.com.br/assunto/porto-maravilha/ (accessed 10 March 2018).

Relatório Reservado (2014b) Trump Towers balançam antes mesmo de sair do chão. Available at: https://relatorioreservado.com.br/assunto/porto-maravilha/ (accessed 10 March 2018).

Relatório Reservado (2014c) Caixa Maravilha. Available at: https://relatorioreservado.com.br/assunto/porto-maravilha/ (accessed 10 March 2018).

Relatório Reservado (2015a): Búlgaros tiram Trump Towers da prancheta. Available at: https://relatorioreservado.com.br/assunto/porto-maravilha/ (accessed 10 March 2018).

Relatório Reservado (2015b) Caixa Econômica. Available at: https://relatorioreservado.com.br/assunto/porto-maravilha/ (accessed 10 March 2018).

Relatório Reservado (2016) Salas vazias. Available at: https://relatorioreservado.com.br/assunto/porto-maravilha/ (accessed 10 March 2018).

Relatório Reservado (2017a) Porto depressão. Available at: https://relatorioreservado.com.br/assunto/porto-maravilha/ (accessed 10 March 2018).

Relatório Reservado (2017b) Cidade-fantasma. Available at: https://relatorioreservado.com.br/assunto/porto-maravilha/ (accessed 10 March 2018).

Relatório Reservado (2017c) Porto fantasma. Available at: https://relatorioreservado.com.br/assunto/tishman-speyer/ (accessed 10 March 2018).

Relatório Reservado (2017d) Legado olímpico. Available at: https://relatorioreservado.com.br/assunto/tishman-speyer/ (accessed 10 March 2018).

Relatório Reservado (2018a) O Rio de Janeiro cobra seu preço. Available at: (accessed 10 March 2018).

Relatório Reservado (2018b) Caixa busca solução para um porto nada maravilha. Available at: https://relatorioreservado.com.br/caixa-busca-uma-solucao-para-um-porto-nada-maravilha/ (accessed 10 March 2018).

Reuters (2017) Governo fecha acordo para recuperação do Rio e ajuste fiscal será de R$63 bi até 2020. Available at: https://br.reuters.com/article/topNews/idBRKCN1BG2NH-OBRTP (accessed 10 March 2018).

Roberts W. C. (2017) What was primitive accumulation? Reconstructing the origin of a critical concept. *European Journal of Political Theory*. Online: first published October 11, 2017. doi: 10.1177/1474885117735961.

Bibliography 111

Roche M. (2000) *Mega-Events and Modernity: Olympics and Expos in the Growth of Global Culture*. New York: Routledge.

Saad Filho A. (2011) Crisis in neoliberalism or crisis of neoliberalism. *Socialist Register* 47: 242–259.

Sanders B. (2011) The Fed Audit US Sanate. Available at: https://www.sanders.senate. gov/newsroom/press-releases/sanders-supports-audit-the-fed-bill (accessed 18 January 2018).

dos Santos Pereira A. L. (2015) *Intervenções em centros urbanos e conflitos distributivos: modelos regulatórios, circuitos de valorização e estratégias discursivas*. Tese (Doutorado em Direito), Universidade de São Paulo, São Paulo.

Sarue B. (2018) Quando grandes projetos urbanos acontecem? Uma análise a partir do Porto Maravilha no Rio de Janeiro. *Dados* 61(3): 581–616.

Sauer S. and Leite P. S. (2012) Agrarian structure foreign investment in land and land prices in Brazil. *The Journal of Peasant Studies* 39(3–4): 873–898.

Schwarcz L. (2012) *A longa viagem da biblioteca dos reis. Do terremoto de Lisboa à independência do Brasil*. São Paulo: Cia das Letras.

Schwarcz L. (2017) O cais do Valongo. *Nexojornal*. Available at: https://www.nexojornal. com.br/colunistas/2017/O-Cais-do-Valongo (accessed 22 January 2018).

Sena Y. (2018) Vamos acabar com coitadismo de nordestino de gay de negro e de mulher diz Bolsonaro. *Folha de S Paulo*, 23 October 2018.

Silva A. (2015) Porto Maravilha: onde passado e futuro se encontram. Available at: https:// portomaravilha.com.br/artigosdetalhes/cod/22 (accessed 22 January 2018).

Silva L. (2003) *História do urbanismo no Rio de Janeiro: administração municipal, engenharia e arquitetura dos anos 1920 à ditadura Vargas*. Rio de Janeiro: E-Papers Serviços Editorias.

da Silva Pereira J. C. M. (2007) *À flor da terra : o cemitério dos pretos novos no Rio de Janeiro*. Rio de Janeiro: IPHAN.

da Silva Pereira J. C. M. (2013) Revisitando o Valongo: mercado de almas, lazareto e cemitério de africanos no portal do Atlântico (a cidade do Rio de Janeiro, no século XIX). *Revista de História Comparada* 7(1): 218–243.

da Silva Soares E. M. A. and Moreira F. D. (2007) Preservação do patrimônio cultural e reabilitação urbana: o caso da zona portuária da cidade do Rio de Janeiro. *Da Vinci* 4(1): 101–120.

Singer A. (2012) *Os sentidos do lulismo: reforma gradual e pacto conservador*. São Paulo: CiA das Letras.

Soares P. R. R. (2013) Megaeventos esportivos e o urbano: a copa do mundo de 2014 e seus impactos nas cidades brasileiras. *Revista FSA* 10: 195–214.

Sobral B. L. B. (2017) Crise no Estado do Rio de Janeiro: diagnóstico e perspectivas. *Revista Econômica* 19(1): 7–34.

Sobral B. L. B. (2018) O sentido histórico da formação econômica fluminense e desdobramentos para a crise de suas finanças públicas estaduais: desafios estruturais diante da estrutura produtiva oca. *Anais do XXIII Encontro Nacional de Economia Política da Sociedade Brasileira de Economia Política*, Niteroi. Available at: http://sep.org.br/ anais/Trabalhos%20para%20o%20site/Area%207/108.pdf (accessed 18 January 2018).

Soederberg S. (2013) Universalising financial inclusion and the securitisation of development. *Third World Quarterly* 34(4): 593–612.

Souza L. M. (1999) *Norma e conflito – Aspectos da história de Minas no século XVIII*. Belo Horizonte: UFMG.

Streeck W. (2015) Wie wird der Kapitalismus enden? *Blätter für deutsche und internationale Politik* 3: 99–111.

112   Bibliography

Streeck W. (2016) *How Will Capitalism End? Essays on a Failing System*. London/New York: Verso.

Tavares R. B. (2012) *Cemitério dos Pretos Novos, Rio de Janeiro, século XIX: uma tentativa de delimitação espacial*. Mestrado, Rio de Janeiro: Museu Nacional.

UOL (2019) Observatório destaca polícia letal em intervenção: "modelo para não copiar". Available at: https://noticias.uol.com.br/cotidiano/ultimas-noticias/2019/02/14/obser vatorio-da-intervencao.htm (accessed 15 February 2019).

Vassallo S. (2015) Culturas em disputa: a criação do programa Porto Maravilha Cultural no projeto de revitalização da região portuária do Rio de Janeiro. In: Pontes G. R. Jr. et al. (eds) *Diálogos interdisciplinares: Literatura e políticas culturais*. Rio de Janeiro: UERJ, pp. 57–82.

Voyages – The Trans-Atlantic Slave Trade Database. Available at: http://www.slavevoyages.org/ (accessed 7 January 2018).

Watts J. (2017) Operation car wash: Is this the biggest corruption scandal in history? *The Guardian*, 1 June 17.

Whitson D. and Horne J. (2006) The glocal politics of sports mega-events: Underestimated costs and overestimated benefits? Comparing the outcomes of sports mega-events in Canada and Japan. *The Sociological Review* 54: 71–89.

Williams D., Chazkel A. and Knauss de Mendonça P. (eds) (2016) *The Rio de Janeiro Reader: History, Culture, Politics*. Durham/London: Duke University Press.

Williams E. (1983 [1944]) *Capitalism and Slavery*, 6th reprint. London: Andre Deutsch.

Witherick M. (1981) Port developments, port-city linkages and prospects for maritime industry: A case study of Southampton. In: Hoyle B. S. and Pinder D. A. (eds) *Cityport Industrialization and Regional Development*. Oxford: Pergamon, pp. 113–132.

Ziesche J., Dämmer L., Natterer M. and Hampf A. (2014) *Mapa das remoções no Rio de Janeiro*. Rio de Janeiro: Heinrich Böll Stiftung. Available at: https://br.boell.org/pt-br/2014/07/03/mapa-das-remocoes-no-rio-de-janeiro (accessed 30 June 2018).

Index

Aberdeen Act (1845) 54
abolition of slavery 22, 29, 61, 100
accumulation: by dispossession 8, 17, 21, 33, 69; capitalist 1, 3, 6, 9, 12–17, 19, 21–22, 23n2, 26, 30–33, 35, 57, 64–66, 72–73, 76, 96–97, 99–100; continuity of 40; dynamic of 2, 13, 21, 26, 30, 42, 65, 97; entangled 3, 5–6, 20–22, 25–26, 30, 42, 48–49, 69, 71–72, 96, 98, 100; expansion of 12; finance 3, 19, 33, 94; global 7, 21, 32, 36, 96; mercantilist 3, 42; necessities of 2; of capital 3, 7–8, 10–12, 26, 30, 33, 42–43, 47, 51, 53, 55n5, 62–65, 72, 90, 99; over- 7, 9, 76–78, 92, 95; overaccumulation 78; pattern of 3, 21, 33, 67, 90; primary 14; primitive 2–4, 6–8, 10–14, 17–18, 20, 27, 34–35, 38–39, 45, 51, 97; productive 11, 15
Alencastro, L. F. 37, 46, 74n4–5
Altvater, E. 80
Andreatta, V. 31, 66
Araujo, K. 78–79
assets 69, 81, 83; fictitious 79–80, 92, 95; generating 69; pecuniary 39; supply of 62
austerity 81, 88; anti- 87; fiscal 60, 86; measures of 86, 88, 90; policies 77, 88; politics of 10; radical measures of 77; regime of 80
authoritarianism 77–79, 82, 89

Backhouse, M. 20, 22
Benchimol, J. L. 29
Bicalho, M. F. 38–40
Bielefeld School 15, 23n7
Blackburn, R. 12
bloody legislation 3, 17, 18
BNDES (State Bank of Development) 83
Bolsonaro, President Jair 77, 82, 84–85, 95

Bolsonaro, Senator F. 89
Brand, C. 50

Cabral, Governor S. 86
Caldeira, J. 37
Cano, W. 59–60
capital, concentration of 6–7, 11, 13, 15
capitalism: contemporary 16; development of 7–9, 10, 14–15, 55n5; dynamics of 2, 11, 100; expansion of 14–15, 22, 33, 40; financial 9, 23n6, 67, 69–71, 78, 97; global 3, 14, 75, 96; history of 4, 7, 80; industrial 7, 12; mercantile 49, 96; neoliberal 4, 10; normalised 14; predatory 14; reproduction of 3; 'vulture' 8; world 34; see also expropriation, value
Cardoso, R. (2015) 30–31, 33n3, 62
carnival 61–62, 68, 73n4, 88
Carvalho, J. M. 44, 77
Carvalho, L. (2019) 77
Car Wash Operation 71, 74n8
CDURP (Company of Urban Development of the Port Region of Rio de Janeiro) 69–70, 92
CEF (Federal Savings Bank) 70, 90–91, 93–94
Cemetery of Pretos Novos 44, 48, 51–52, 54, 68, 98
CEPAC (Certificates of Additional Construction Potential) 69–71, 75, 90–95
Chesnais, M. 94
Church 17, 27–28, 53, 58, 98; Anglican 17; Catholic 17, 27
Ciata, Tia 61–62
Cislaghi, J. F. 86, 90
colonial: economy 96; expansion 7, 15, 33; exploitation 12, 23n2, 24n9; State 17–19; society 54

114 Index

colonialism 11–13, 17–18
commodification 2–3, 15, 18, 67, 77, 92–93, 98–99; hyper 82; multinational 67; potential 23n2; processes 40; re- 2, 77, 90, 95
commodity 36–37, 76; boom 85; collapse of price 85; commercialised 35; exchange 7; market 32; slave 36; *see also* crisis
Conde, Mayor L. P. 31
Conrad, S. 21
corruption 20, 22, 71, 74n8, 77, 83–84, 86–87, 90; allegations 84; scandals 20, 77, 86
Costa, S. 21, 84
crisis: Brazilian 82; commodity 86; debt 59, 77; economic 3, 70, 76, 97; financial 80–82, 90; fiscal 77; global 59, 77, 79, 81–82, 88; international 85; legitimation 78; Lehman Brother 76; liquidity 81; national 77, 88; overaccumulation 78, 92, 95; political 3, 97; Rio de Janeiro 85, 89, 92
Crivella, Mayor M. 94–95
culture 22–23, 61, 68, 72; Afrodescendent 61–62, 99; black 64; Brazilian 61; Catalonian 67; European 46, 61; local 63, 68, 99; material 2; mobilisation of 98; producers of 72; urban 25; Western 64
Cunha, President of Chamber of Deputy E. 42, 71

Darwin, C. 50
debt 10, 59, 94; banking 89; burden 80; contracted 59; external 60; future 94; Greek 8; high 82; public 60, 88–90; *see also* crisis
decommodification 2, 65, 75, 92, 95, 97, 99
degradation 1, 53, 68, 81; continual 55
degraded: areas 20, 99; land 20; space 1, 65, 68, 96, 99; tenement houses 31; urban environment 97
deindustrialisation 60, 76, 82, 85
democracy 78, 81–82
demographic 40; vacuum 1–2, 71; void 75
devaluation 53–54, 60
disciplining 18, 42, 45, 49
dispossession 8–11, 17, 19, 21, 79, 89; of cities 67; of common land 78; of families 10; *see also* accumulation
Dornelles, Governor F. 87
Dörre, K. 4, 8–11, 14, 17, 19, 20, 22, 23n2, 45, 80

economic: activities 9, 32, 43, 59, 84; agents 36, 83; consequences 81; deceleration 60; depletion 30; duress 14; enterprise 49, 52; environment 19; expansion 40, 53; expectations 1, 90; exploitation 9, 72; growth 76, 83; losses 51; momentum 43; movement 52; policies 82; powers 80, 82; recession 76, 85, 89–90, 92; relations 33, 94; sectors 22, 36, 76; significance 59; socio- 22, 82, 92; *see also* crisis, violence
Ekman, F. 16
enslaved 98, 100; Africans 2, 34, 37, 47–49, 96, 100; black population 43, 100; black women 46; humans 12; individuals 49; labourers 27, 39; people 52; persons 2, 34–36
entangled: capitalist expropriations 96; inequalities 21, 22; modernity 21; *see also* accumulation
European: banking families 29; civilisatory ideal 64; colonial powers 19; Commission 80; consumer goods 32; culture 46, 61; Enlightenment, 12; industry 33, 35; manufactured goods 32; metropolis 4; national economies 12; Union 80
Eusébio de Queiroz Law 52, 55
expansion: capitalist 3, 7, 8, 12, 14, 19–21, 23n2, 40, 78, 96; colonial 7, 15, 33; continual 6; external 11; imperial 3, 14; industrial 35, 59; mercantile 40; Napoleonic 28; of authoritarian rules 78; of economic activities 84; urban 30, 43; *see also* accumulation, capitalism, economic
exploitation 7, 11, 15, 42, 71–72; economic 9; extreme 13; *see also* colonial, superexploitation
exports 43, 60, 65, 76; agricultural 57, 59; coffee 28, 97; commodities 62, 76; manufacturing goods 35; meat 83; of colonial products 97; of primary products 34, 58, 65; sugar 27, 97
expropriation 7, 9–11, 14–20, 33, 36, 38–39, 42, 45, 71, 73, 77–81, 86–90, 93, 95, 97–100: capitalist 2, 4, 8, 16, 19, 23n6, 87, 96; continuous 7; cycle of 77–78, 81–82; financial 22; multiple 15; object of 17, 36; of nature 15, 22; of rights 81; permanent 10; policy of 86; primary 81; secondary 15, 16, 22, 33; theory of 5; unlimited 90; violent 92; *see also* dynamic

Index 115

Fairweather, C. 16
far-right 78, 82, 97
favela 61, 87, 89–90; removal of 67
FGTS (Workers' Social Security Fund)
70–72, 93
Figueiredo, C. 27, 27, 41, 63
FIIP (Real Estate Investment Fund of the
Port Region) 69, 71, 91–94
financialisation 10–11, 23n6, 33, 59–60,
76, 92
Fiscal Recovery Regime 77, 88
Florentino, M. 34–37, 44, 47
Fonseca, P. C. 57–58
Fontes, V. 14–15, 22, 23n6
Football World Cup (2014) 66, 86
Fordist period 19
Franco, M. S. de C. 34
Franco, Marielle 77, 89
Frank, A. G. 12–14, 22
Freireyss, G. W. 50–51
Fridman, F. 17, 26, 28, 31–32, 58
Furtado, C. 34

Gaffney, C. 67
global: circuits of production 75; city 27;
commercial networks 27; demands 62;
division of labour 12; economy 27, 30,
64–65, 96; empire 46; financial capital
76; impulse 45; map of power relations
45; market 14, 27, 67, 76; North 15;
perspective 22; production 10; scale
10; social inequalities 21; South 4, 15,
81; slave trade 37; stage 8; tendency of
dispossession 67; tourist market 63, 97;
see also accumulation, capitalism, crisis,
dynamic
Gonçalves, G. L. 76–78, 80, 88–90
Góngora-Mera, M. 19
Gorender, J. 34
government 22, 46, 60, 62, 70, 80, 83–86,
88, 90, 99; agencies 90; bonds 76, 89;
Brazilian 20; coalitions 76; Federal
31, 61, 63–64, 77, 88, 90, 97; local 97;
military 59; Rio de Janeiro 86–87, 90,
97; State 86, 88; transfers 87–88; United
States 80
green grabbing (*grüne Landnahme*) 20

Haag, C. 43–44, 51, 53
Harvey, D. 8–11, 14, 17, 19–21, 67, 77
Haubner, T. 15, 23n7
Honorato, C. P. 27, 40, 42–44, 48–51,
53–54, 56n10

ICMS (Value Added Tax) 86
illegal(ity) 22, 89, 97; activities 41;
commerce 38, 40–41; importation 37;
money 87; negotiations 83; purchase of
slaves 37; trade 41–42, 54; usurpation 18
Imperatriz Wharf 55, 68, 73, 100
import 59–60, 65, 97; goods 32, 34, 37–38,
59, 65; illegal 37; legal 37; slave 51, 54;
stimulating 60
independence 22, 28, 31, 46–47, 57
Industrial Revolution 13
industrialisation 3, 11, 58–59, 65
inequalities 21, 82; social 21; *see also*
entangled
infrastructure 9, 19, 30, 54, 66, 84;
extended 69; investments 30, 71; limited
45; precarious 61; projects 2, 64, 69–70
interpenetration 12, 21–22, 33, 46, 100
intervention 31, 47, 55, 67, 69, 88, 90, 99;
disciplinary 99; federal in Rio de Janeiro
77, 88–90; political 18; public 62;
regulatory 7–8, 17, 19, 40, 98; sanitary
45, 48–49; state 8, 22, 59, 92; urban 1,
33n3, 75
investment 8–9, 19, 30, 33, 35–36, 58,
67, 71, 85, 90–91, 93; agencies 80;
availability of 59; capitalist 65; financial
market 60; groups 11; high 87; of
surplus capital 9; opportunities 91;
private 67; productive 60; public 9, 67,
77; real estate 1, 67; state 9; suspension
of 3; *see also* infrastructure
IOC (International Olympic Committee) 1
ISI (import substitution industrialisation)
59, 65

Knox, R. 19

labour-power 7, 9, 11–13, 18, 23, 58, 98
Lamarão, S. T. N. 27, 38, 40, 42–43
Land Act (1850) 57–58
Lavinas, L. 4, 76, 78, 89
Lavradio, Marquis of 42–44, 47, 53
law: civil 20; economic 7; environmental
71, 84; international 19; labour 19; penal
18–20, 51–52, 98; urban 20
Lazarette of Valongo 47–48, 53, 56n8
legal(ity) 22, 69, 81, 89, 97; activities 41;
alterations 31; changes 3; characteristics
23; commerce 38; conditions 31; form
of contract 15; historical- 18; imports
37; instruments 19; liberalism 82;
negotiations 83; –political discourse 51;

116 Index

reforms 19; regime 38, 49, 57; status 22; usurpation 18
Lemos, G. de 4, 26
Lessa, C. 76–77
Lima, T. A. 2, 28, 30, 34, 48, 55, 72
Little Africa 60–61, 63, 68
Lula da Silva, President L. I. 82
lulismo 82–84, 95n2
Luxemburg, R. 3, 7–8, 14, 21, 23n2, 23n7, 32, 98

Maia, Mayor C. 31
Marini, R. M. 12
market: capitalist 58; consumer 33; economy 8; financial 19, 60; integrated commodity 32; internal 29, 37; international 76–77; labour 9; land 58; meat 2; protection 38; real estate 36, 64, 66, 75–76, 90–95, 99; slave 21, 28, 34, 43–44, 48–49, 53–54, 96; stock 59; tourist 63; value 71, 99; world 63; see also global
Marx, K. 2–3, 6–8, 10–15, 17–20, 21, 32, 97
Marxist: affirmations 17; feminists 15; political economy 3, 6, 7, 18; theory 3
modernisation 14, 46, 62, 68; classical 72; projects 63, 87; technological 64; theory 75; urban 29
Moreira, C. C. 65–66
Moura, R. 27, 61–62, 73n3
museum 46, 67, 72; Art of Rio de Janeiro (MAR) 68; of Tomorrow (Museu do Amanhã) 68, 75, 100

Nascimento, A. P. 61
Norcliffe, G. 25

Oliveira, A. 59–60, 87
Olympics (2016) 1, 19, 66–67, 75, 85–87; Boulevard 67; City 87; Park 87
Operation Unfair Play 1

Paes, Mayor E. 1, 31, 67, 68, 70, 75, 94, 99
Passos, Mayor P. 30, 55, 62–65, 74n5, 99
Pereira, L. 43–44, 48–49, 50–51, 53–55, 61
Pezão, Governor L. F. 86–87
Pijning, E. (2001) 40–42
Pinto, Governor General R. V. 38–39, 43
political: actions 69, 79; articulation 61; core 86; –cultural production 65; decisions 20, 37, 82, 98; depletion 30; discourse 51, 97; economists 3, 34;

forces 76; instability 76; motivation 17, 89; opportunities 72; organisation 61, 64; points of view 30, 73, 83; power 82; preferences 85; –regulatory 20; representation 82; –state dimension 8; systems 78, 81–82; tensions 82; violence 8, 17, 77, 95, 100; world 25; see also crisis, intervention, Marxist
port–city: confluence 43; relation 42; symbiotic trajectory 25–26
Porto Maravilha (Marvellous Port) 32, 67–68, 70, 72–73, 75, 87, 93, 95, 99; magazine 1; project 1, 3–4, 66–71, 73, 75, 90–92, 94, 97–99
Porto Novo Concessionary 70–71, 74n7, 75, 91, 94–95
Pradella, L. 10
Prado, Júnior C. 34
privatisation 9, 10, 15, 19, 22, 73, 78, 81–82, 84, 88–90
property: common 18; imperatives of 11; monopolised 15; private 7, 98; right to 19, 39; sales of 40; state 57
protests 54, 76, 78, 81, 87–88; country-wide 77; criminalisation of 77, 88; cycle of 87; mass 82; social 88, 90
public–private partnerships 17, 19–20, 40, 48–49, 98

Ramos, S. 88, 90
Randeria, S. 21
real estate 16, 30, 64, 66–67, 70, 72, 92, 99; bubbles 10, 77; buildings 91; business 93; capital 98–99; companies 91–93; corporations 90; developments 75; interest in 66; investments 1, 67; operators 66; sector 91; units 70; wealth 80; see also market
reform 21, 62–64, 67–68, 91, 93, 98–99; Anglican 17; future 64; legal 19; pension system 81; port 29; projects 29; tax 84; urban 2, 21, 31, 55, 63–65, 68, 71, 75, 86, 90, 93, 98
regulation 8, 9, 18–19, 23, 31, 37–38, 47, 78
re-primarisation 76
resources 8, 16, 19, 38, 69–71, 87, 92–95; discursive 98; financial 69; motivational 78; natural 15, 81; speculative 97; state 3, 20, 84, 89, 97
revitalisation 1, 67–68, 72, 91
Revolt: Malê (1835) 47; of the Lash 61; Vaccine 61
Roberts, W. C. 14, 17

Index 117

Rodrigues, A. 59–60
Rodrigues Alves, President 29, 55,
 62–64, 98
Rousseff, President Dilma, 82;
 impeachment of 83

Saad Filho, A. 80
samba 61, 63, 68
Schwarcz, L. M. 46
settlement 25–26, 28, 47; Portuguese 26;
 urban 25
Singer, A. 82
slave: market 28, 43–44, 48–49, 53–54,
 96; trade 12, 28, 34–37, 43, 46, 48–50,
 54–55, 56n11, 57–58, 60, 97–98
Sobral, B. L. B.76–77, 85–86, 89
Soederberg, S. 70
Souza, L. M. 19
space: commodified 3, 9, 77, 89; degraded
 1, 65, 68, 96; non-capitalist 7, 33, 100;
 non-commodified 9–10, 17, 20–21, 26,
 71, 96–98
State violence 77, 79, 81, 88, 90
Strangford Treaty (1810) 12, 23n5
Streeck, W. 81–82
superexploitation 12–13, 22
symbiotic trajectory 25–26, 42

Tavares, R. B. 27, 39, 48–50, 52–54
Temer, President M. 84, 88
Trump Towers 91–92

urban: centre 26; culture 25; designs
 23; development 42; dynamic 71;
 environment 97; equipment 19;
 expansion 30, 43, 53; fabric 25, 67;
 functions 65; governance 75; hegemonic
 objectives 69; labour 38, 42; law 20;
 layout 29; modernisation 29; nucleus
 31; policies 54; population 29; practices
 63; projects 43, 75; rearrangement
 58; reforms 2, 21, 29, 31, 55, 63–65,

68, 71, 75, 86, 90, 93, 98; refuse 53;
 renewal 30, 32, 63–64; renovation
 75; restructuring 66, 98; settlements
 25; space 28–29, 39, 59; system 25,
 67; terrain 31; territories 64–65;
 transportation 29; vacuum 72; *see also*
 interventions
UNESCO (United Nations Educational,
 Scientific and Cultural Organization) 2
usurpation 17–19

Valongo 2, 29, 32, 40, 43–44, 48–49,
 51, 53–54, 62, 72; complex 28, 45,
 54; district of 31, 48, 54; Lazarette of
 47–48, 53, 56n8, 56n10; warehouse of
 50; Wharf 31, 43, 55, 68, 73, 100
value: capitalist 2, 7; commercial 16, 60;
 creation 1; cultural 2; economic 87;
 enormous 36; generation of 26; market
 1, 71, 99; moral 95; production 25,
 30, 62, 65, 97; surplus 3, 6–8, 11–14,
 16, 20, 23n6, 33; symbolic 72;
 unitary 95
Vargas, President G. 30
Vassallo, S. 30, 68, 72
violence 7, 17, 36, 39, 47, 54, 77, 87, 95;
 aesthetical 95; archaic 14; authoritarian
 95; cycle of 88; explicit 8, 15, 97;
 increase in 88; lawless 89; non-
 economic 3, 7, 17; of financialisation
 10; permanent 10; simulated 7; symbolic
 99; *see also* political, State

War of Canudos 61, 73n1
wealth 16, 25, 28, 36, 41, 46, 60, 65–66,
 68, 73, 83; concentration of 81;
 housing 80; immense 10; real estate 80;
 redistribution of 10; Republic's 76
Williams, D. 26–27, 41, 44, 47, 52
Williams, E. 12
Witzel, Governor Wilson 77
WTO (World Trade Organisation) 22

Printed in the United States
By Bookmasters